'We are entering a period of great transition – stormy times of uncertainty, threat and possibility, which will especially affect the lives of young people – yet guides to the future for educators and their students are woefully few. David Hicks's new book is timely, significant, and necessarily bold – a criticall...
make to...
and an i...

Prof...

'In this...
issue...
provi...
"know,...
with c...
Troubl...
parent...
about y...

Dr Bro...

'Fo...
pre...
peopl...
in Trou...
need

Tim Grant, Edit...

'Once again, David Hicks provides the premier educational perspective on important global issues and trends. For over thirty years, whether the concern is su... young people's yearning for a positive future or the climate... and the art of teaching like no other. This is a must-read book for every teacher seeking to understand the defining issue of the twenty-first century and how to practise *Educating for Hope in Troubled Times*.'

Professor John Fien, Executive Director, Swinburne Leadership Institute, Melbourne

'As always, Hicks makes the most complex issues accessible for developing understandings in the classroom, as well as for professional learning. He connects the important role of education with its powerful capacity to enable students to prepare for unknown futures. More importantly, this book provides a powerful and positive message through action, to disrupt dominant messages of doom and gloom associated with climate change.'

Debra Bateman, Associate Professor, School of Education, Deakin University, Australia

'It is more than four decades since the emergence of growing awareness about the global environmental crisis, and education systems have yet to develop robust and urgent responses. Throughout this time David Hicks has been at the cutting edge of attempts to help educators understand these issues and develop practical and hopeful strategies for working with children and young people. This book is a testament to his thinking and imagination as a teacher and hopeful traveller in search of a better world. It deserves to be read by all teachers concerned about how to help children and young people make sense of the post-carbon futures that await them.'

Professor John Morgan, School of Curriculum and Pedagogy, University of Auckland, New Zealand

Educating for Hope in Troubled Times

IOEPress   *tb* Trentham Books

School curricula have generally reflected poorly upon a sense of urgency toward social, economic, or cultural issues, let alone to ever increasing environmental degradation and global climate change.
Chronicles from a Watershed: Consideration of place and pedagogy
Nelson and Brodie (2011)

Educating for Hope in Troubled Times

Climate change and the transition to a post-carbon future

David Hicks

A Trentham Book
Institute of Education Press

First published in 2014 by the Institute of Education Press, University of London, 20 Bedford Way, London WC1H 0AL
ioepress.co.uk

British Library Cataloguing in Publication Data:
A catalogue record for this publication is available from the British Library

ISBNs
978-1-85856-553-8 (paperback)
978-1-85856-628-3 (PDF eBook)
978-1-85856-629-0 (ePub eBook)
978-1-85856-630-6 (Kindle eBook)

Typeset by Quadrant Infotech (India) Pvt Ltd
Printed by CPI Group (UK) Ltd, Croydon, CR0 4YY

Cover photo: Ashden Awards/Energy4All Fens Cooperative. Panel installation (p. 15) www.davidmchugh.co.uk. Other images (pp. 64, 105, 148) Andrew Aitchison/Ashden Awards.
Box 1.1 (p. 22) is reproduced by kind permission of UKCIP.
Box 2.1 (p. 34); Activities 1–5 in Box 2.3 (pp. 46–7); Box 6.2 (p. 98); and Box 8.3 (pp. 127–8) are from *The Transition Handbook* by Rob Hopkins, and are reproduced by kind permission of Green Books, **www.greebooks.co.uk**
Figure 2.1 (p. 37) is reproduced by kind permission of ASPO International.
Box 3.2 (pp. 61–2) is adapted from 'How big is your footprint?' (2002), Second Nature, RSPB Scotland, and reproduced by kind permission of WWF Scotland.
Box 5.1 (pp. 80–81) is from 'The future only arrives when things look dangerous', by David Hicks. Reproduced by kind permission of Elsevier.
Figure 6.1 (p. 102) is from *Sustainable Schools, Sustainable Futures*, and is reproduced by kind permission of WWF UK.
Box 8.1 (pp. 123–4) is reproduced by kind permission of Action for Sustainable Living.
Box 9.1 (pp. 135–6) © Forum for the Future. Reproduced by permission.
Box 10.2 (pp. 158–9) is reproduced by kind permission of Post-Carbon Living.
Box 11.2 (pp. 168–9) is reproduced by kind permission of Dr David Selby.
Figure 11.1 (p. 174) is reproduced by kind permission of Dr Martha Rogers.

Contents

To all those working towards a post-carbon future

Acknowledgements

In troubled times it seems important to stand back in order to get some purchase on the bigger picture. How did we get to this place? Where does it seem we're going? What might we want to do about this? And yet in order to gain some sort of overview it is friends, family and colleagues that sustain and encourage us. Many people have supported me directly and indirectly in the writing of this book and deeply deserve my gratitude and thanks. They are as follows.

John Morgan introduced me to the notion of a 'post-carbon curriculum' and Bob Digby invited me to lecture to the Geographical Association on 'A Geography of Hope'. Robin Richardson inspired me in educational matters progressive and radical right from the start. Only after completing the book did I realize I was indebted to him for its main title. I thank Patrick Whitaker, who gave me unstinting support throughout our long friendship. Cathie Holden and Nick Clough always kept me in the loop during our supportive lunches and Kay Wood and Andy Bord encouraged both personal and professional reflection on our various excursions. Les and Mike kept me walking throughout the seasons and Lou gave me the space to get on with things however long it might take. My grandchildren, Holly and Ethan, are an essential part of the picture because it's their possible futures that I write about.

For many years the School of Education at Bath Spa University gave me the space in which to teach and research as the spirit moved me and I also thank here all those who were involved in my Hawkwood conferences. Other key figures to whom I owe a deep gratitude are those who have specifically influenced and inspired my work. These include David Orr, who showed me the educational task; Joanna Macy and Chris Johnstone for their dedication to the Great Turning; sociologist John Urry for his critical insights on mobilities and peak oil; Richard Heinberg and his commitment to exploring and explaining the nature of transition; Bronwyn Hayward for reminding me what citizenship has become and what it needs to be; Rob Hopkins and the Transition Movement for working to put things into practice; David Selby and Fumiyo Kagawa for always pushing the boundaries.

Thank you all for being important sources of hope in my life and work.

David Hicks
Chepstow
January 2014

About the author

David Hicks is a freelance educator and formerly Professor in the School of Education, Bath Spa University, where he helped develop and taught on the undergraduate Education Studies degree. For the last thirty years his research, writing and teaching have focused on ways of helping students and teachers think more critically and creatively about the future. He has published widely in the fields of geography education, global education and futures education, and has a particular interest in education for sustainability, climate change, and the shift to a post-carbon future. His publications include *Sustainable Schools, Sustainable Futures: A resource for teachers*; *Teaching the Global Dimension: Key principles and effective practice*; *Lessons for the Future: The missing dimension in education* and *Citizenship for the Future: A practical classroom guide*. Further details of his work can be found at: www.teaching4abetterworld.co.uk

Foreword

Education is an essential function of civilization. Its essence is simple: to equip the young for the many tasks of preserving and advancing the hard-won gains of humankind in the arts, sciences and humanities. To the extent that any generation succeeds in this aim, then the next is better able to meet its own needs and anchor itself in some larger mythos and system of values.

Beneath this simple description, however, is endless complexity and controversy. Who is qualified to teach? What should the young be taught? How should they learn? Should they be taught critical thinking or obedience to authority? What is the proper role of classroom learning relative to experiential learning? Should education be aimed for specific skills or breadth? What is the relationship between facts and values, or between information and wisdom? How do various disciplines relate to each other, or do they relate at all? Is education a proper public goal or should it be left to families and civic organizations? Is there a common core of factual knowledge? What does it mean to teach young people to think, or to think about the *act* of thinking? Is smartness overrated relative, say, to qualities of compassion, sociability, character and manual competence? And so we could go on.

Reasonable answers to these age-old questions are more difficult in the electronic world. Schools, colleges and universities are only part of the educational apparatus of the postmodern age. Television, the internet and social media spread by ubiquitous small, mobile devices now play an equivalent – or larger – role in shaping postmodern minds than does formal education. Ideas and information of all sorts move more quickly than ever before and with less editing and filtering, and so they could be said to remain relatively untainted by what once passed for reflective judgement and wisdom. The result is a tsunami of data, imagery, messaging, manipulative advertising, information and chatter inundating young minds and shattering attention into a thousand (mostly commercially exploitable) shards. Educators, curriculum planners and administrators, many of whom have found themselves caught flat footed, have yet to catch up with a rapidly changing reality.

If the speed and volume of information were not enough of a challenge, the global outlook for the rising generation and their descendants is also not rosy. By one estimate we already consume the Earth's renewable bounty by an excess of 50 per cent and consumption continues to rise, pushing 'overshoot day' (the day each year when we cross the 100 per cent renewability threshold) earlier each year. Climate will continue to destabilize for hundreds or thousands of years. The consequences will leave no part of the world unaffected. Oceans are warming and acidifying. Species will die out in large numbers. Ecosystems will be increasingly threadbare and stressed. And yet the leadership necessary to forestall the worst that could happen is criminally negligent, giving rise to pessimism as to whether anything can be done and to cynicism about politics, business – and education for that matter. What do we tell young people, instinctively optimistic in their glands and genes, about their future? How does the hard scientific reality fit into the curriculum? What should they know? How and when should it be taught? Indeed, as David Hicks asks, how do we keep hope – rather than wishful thinking – alive in the 'long emergency' ahead?

The question has no single answer. Indeed, it may not have any *good* answers. But we are not without good starting points. The first is that the disorder in the outside world reflects an inner disorder of how we think. That makes it the business of educators to better calibrate the curriculum with ecological realities. Second, environmental education often exists as a kind of outhouse tacked on to the main building where supposedly the really important business of education resides. But all education is implicitly environmental education. 'By what we include or exclude we teach young people that they are part of or apart from nature' (Orr, 1994). Ecology, thermodynamics and environment ought to be woven throughout the entire curriculum, and not dealt with as side issues or in the recesses of the curriculum. Third, the implication is clear: education is not just another line on our 'to do' list but, rather, the linchpin that connects all of the others together. Our predicament is first and foremost a crisis *of* education, not one *in* education. Fourth, it will not be enough to acquaint students with the science portraying the vital signs of Earth without also enabling them to understand the causes that lie in the humanities and social sciences. Equally important, students should acquire a working knowledge of the new transdisciplinary fields of ecological economics, biomimicry, ecological design, natural systems agriculture, ecologically based planning, and environmental ethics. Finally, we know that we're not likely to do much to save anything that we do not love. Educators ought, then, to engage students in nature by way of field trips, outdoor learning activities – and simply spending time among woods, fields, riversides and seashores. The benefits, as Richard Louv has explained in *The Last Child in the Woods* (2005) and other works, are many, including better health, clearer minds and the kind of inspiration that comes only from our innate affinity for life.

We are not, in other words, without good reason for hope and good cause to act accordingly. In contrast to optimism or despair, hope is a 'verb with its sleeves rolled up'. It demands that we do something. The role of educators, as David Hicks explains here, is to fortify hope and give young people the wherewithal to act with competence, imagination and courage. The 'troubled times' ahead give us no good reason to believe in quick victories but every reason to work towards a better world and look towards the farther horizon.

David W. Orr
Paul Sears Distinguished Professor of Environmental Studies and Politics
Oberlin College, USA

Introduction:
Thinking globally

A challenging world

As a young teacher in the 1970s I watched a TV documentary entitled *Due to Lack of Interest Tomorrow Has Been Cancelled*. I certainly did not wish that to be the case and this has been reflected in much of my work since then. One of the things I discovered was the existence of a long-standing tradition in education that stresses the importance of helping young people understand the interdependence of local and global community. Over the last twenty years or so this has increasingly focused on understanding issues of environment, citizenship and sustainability.

The crucial importance of these concerns was highlighted by the first Earth Summit, held in Rio de Janeiro in 1992, which stressed the interdependence of human and planetary well-being and the need therefore to develop and pursue practices that were sustainable rather than unsustainable. If something is sustainable it can continue beneficially over a long period of time. Conversely, if something is unsustainable it is hazardous to the health and well-being of people and planet. Much of the debate over the intervening twenty years has been about how rich-world lifestyles, in particular, need to change in order to help create a more just and sustainable global future (Visser, 2009a, 2009b). Issues such as record greenhouse gas emissions, melting Arctic sea ice, natural disasters and extreme weather events continue to be regularly reported in the news. Are issues such as these to be avoided in school or should education have a key role to play in helping young people reflect critically on such matters? If one of the aims of education is to prepare young people for the future, how well are we doing that? I ask because key commentators have highlighted a number of major issues lying ahead that urgently require our attention.

Global warnings

Here are three illustrative warnings, the first from Professor John Beddington, recently the UK government's Chief Scientific Adviser. He has cautioned that in the years ahead:

> A 'perfect storm' of food shortages, scarce water and insufficient energy resources threaten to unleash public unrest, cross-border conflicts and mass migration as people flee from the worst-affected regions ... We head into a perfect storm in 2030, because all these things are operating on the same time frame.
>
> (Sample, 2009)

Dr James Hansen, one of the world's leading scientists on climate issues, points out that major climate changes can occur as the result of quite small influences. Extreme dangers can thus arise from global warming, especially when there is a huge gap between official and public knowledge:

> Once ice sheet disintegration begins in earnest, our grandchildren will live the rest of their lives in a chaotic transition period. This transition period necessarily will last several decades ... Business-as-usual greenhouse gas emissions, without any doubt ... will lead eventually to an ice-free planet. An ice-free planet means a sea level rise of about 75 meters (almost 250 feet).
>
> (Hansen, 2011: 250)

Professor David Orr, a leading writer on environment and education, warns of a 'long emergency' that lies ahead as society has to face up to the twin hazards of climate change and peak oil:

> The challenges ahead will be far more difficult than the public has been led to believe and than most of our present leadership apparently understands. Despite the considerable progress in raising awareness of climate change, we are still in a 'consensus trance,' oblivious to the full scope, scale, severity, and duration of the climate destabilisation that is already under way.
>
> (Orr, 2009: 5)

In the past I would not have included such challenging statements in the opening chapter of a book, but would have left them until nearer the end. They need to come here, however, because this book is about just such challenges and the crucial role education can play in helping prepare for them.

A government scientific adviser, a prominent climate scientist and a leading educational writer are all worth listening to, for they also represent much wider bodies of opinion. Perhaps they are only partially right but, whichever way, this book sets out to explore the societal and educational implications of such views, as it is always better to be forewarned rather than to be caught out. Three major global dilemmas and their possible consequences for industrial society are explored in the following chapters – climate change, peak oil and limits to growth. I am aware that a number of other interconnected issues confront global society, such as water scarcity, inequality, malnutrition and species extinction, but here these will only be mentioned in passing.

Climate change arising from global warming is the best known of these issues. Investigated by scientists for some 25 years, the consensus of opinion, as reported by the Intergovernmental Panel on Climate Change, is that such change occurs as the result of human activity on the planet. The irony is that the wealth of the twentieth century was built on the burning of fossil fuels to create energy and the use of its by-products in every aspect of daily life. Yet the effects of past and present global warming, caused by the burning of fossil fuels, will last for centuries and alter every aspect of our lives (Henson, 2011).

Closely related to this problem is the dilemma of peak oil. Global oil production is due to peak sometime around now or in the near future due to its immense demand, both as a fuel and in the creation of fertilizers, chemicals and a wide variety of materials. It seems unlikely that further major oilfields will be discovered. We are therefore approaching the end of what is known as 'easy oil'. There is still oil to be found, but it lies in dangerously deep waters in the Arctic, or else its extraction, as in the case of the Athabasca tar sands in Canada, is likely to cause significant environmental damage. Oil will eventually become less abundant, more costly and more fought over. What alternative fuels will be needed in order to help create a post-carbon future (Buchan, 2010)?

The term 'limits to growth' recognizes that we live in a finite system and that the biosphere – the land, water and air that support all of life – cannot be indefinitely plundered or used as a sink for our wastes. The notion of constant growth as somehow being synonymous with progress has led to extensive environmental and human damage, with the rampant consumerism of the rich world creating a dangerous and impossible norm. While technological developments can resolve some resource problems we still need to learn to live sustainably within ecological limits. The fact that this is not the norm will also alter many aspects of our lives in the future (McKibben, 2010).

It is because global issues such as these are interrelated that John Beddington talks of a 'perfect storm' occurring in the years ahead. The signs of such change are already occurring globally and locally and will continue in the future. This is why commentators such as David Orr (2009) expect the world to be changed dramatically and permanently throughout the course of the twenty-first century. Different parts of the world will be affected in different ways, but essentially we need to move as quickly as possible towards a zero carbon society. There are already many excellent examples of such initiatives occurring and some are reported on in this book. The scope of the changes that will be necessary in our communities, however, suggests that we are entering a long period of challenging transition.

If the commentators reported on here turn out to be wrong then these problems may not be as serious as they seem. However, a 'business as usual' scenario for the future is unlikely. If these commentators are partly, let alone largely, right, then action needs to be taken now in our schools and communities to prepare for that future. This is the new frontier for those who care about young people and the world they will inherit. Non-action is not a viable option.

Good practice in schools

Over the last forty years education has played a significant role in helping young people understand all sorts of local-global issues relating to human and environmental well-being, both in curriculum subject areas and under umbrella terms such as 'global citizenship', 'education for sustainable development' and 'sustainable schools' (Hicks, 2012a). There is a wealth of expertise available to support teachers and educators in handling such matters professionally and competently. It is important to note, however, that different governments view the curriculum in different ways and often dismantle what their predecessors have created, however good that practice may have been. Over the last forty years, therefore, governments have varied in their support for what is sometimes called the 'global dimension in the curriculum'. But educators need to take the long view and be aware of what best practice looks like, whether politicians currently view it to be so or not. The nature of best practice in schools should be decided by professional educators rather than politicians.

The importance and success of the work we are concerned with here is illustrated by four extracts from what were previously official documents. What they say is of crucial importance in itself and also because currently such official educational documentation is largely lacking in England. They are inspirational statements, to which teachers can still aspire.

The notion that global interdependence and sustainability have a vital part to play in schools and teacher education was endorsed in guidelines for teachers entitled *Cross-curriculum Dimensions: A planning guide for schools* (QCA, 2009). This document acknowledged that several issues are of such importance that they should be seen as cross-curricular dimensions rather than relating to just one subject area. The issues included healthy lifestyles, identity and cultural diversity and, in particular, the 'global dimension and sustainable development': *see* Box 0.1.

BOX 0.1 – GLOBAL DIMENSION AND SUSTAINABLE DEVELOPMENT

Learning about [the] global dimension and sustainable development can help young people to understand the needs and rights of present and future generations, and to consider the best ways to tackle climate change, inequality and poverty. It can also motivate learners to want to change things for the better – equipping them with the knowledge, skills and values that are crucial to envisaging and creating a sustainable future. The global dimension and sustainable development engages pupils critically with the following three questions:

- What are the biggest challenges facing our planet and how might they alter its future?
- How can I enjoy a good quality of life, without transferring problems to people in other parts of the world?
- How can I become an active global citizen and help look after the planet for future generations?

Source: QCA (2009: 22)

This is one of the clearest official statements highlighting the need for, and importance of, a global dimension in the curriculum. It also stresses the importance of learning about sustainability issues and in just a few words captures the essence of these concerns and why they should be an essential element in any definition of good education.

Detailed guidance for schools on how to promote sustainability in the curriculum, on campus and in the community, had previously been set out in a document entitled *Planning a Sustainable School* (DCSF, 2008), which is one of the clearest official statements stressing the need for schools to model sustainable practices in their everyday life: *see* Box 0.2. Although it is no longer offered as part of 'official' guidance, many schools still use it as a template for good practice in learning for sustainability.

Box 0.2 – Sustainable schools

Schools have a special role to play in preparing young people to build a brighter future

As places of learning, they can help pupils understand our impact on the planet and encourage them to weigh up the evidence for themselves. As models of good practice, they can offer young people the chance to contribute to sustainable living, and demonstrate good practice to others. Empowering young people to take responsibility for their own future is not only desirable: it is a crucial feature of their education.

A National Framework has been established to guide schools towards this aim

It comprises three interlocking parts:

A commitment to care

Sustainable schools have a caring ethos – care for oneself, for each other (across cultures, distances and generations), and for the environment (far and near). Schools are already caring places, but a sustainable school extends this commitment into new areas. It cares about the energy and water it consumes, the waste it produces, the food it serves, the traffic it attracts, and the difficulties faced by people living in its community and in other parts of the world.

An integrated approach

A sustainable school takes an integrated approach to its improvement. It explores sustainable development through its teaching provision and learning (*curriculum*); in its values and ways of working (*campus*); and in its engagement of local people and partners (*community*).

A selection of 'doorways' or sustainability themes

The doorways are entry points, or places where schools can establish or develop their sustainability practices. Each of the doorways draws its inspiration from a range of national priorities around sustainable development. NB These suggested doorways are: food and drink, energy and water, travel and traffic, purchasing and waste, buildings and grounds, inclusion and participation, local well-being, global dimension.

Source: DCSF (2008: 4–6)

The National College for School Leadership, in its review of research on *Leading Sustainable Schools* (Jackson, L., 2007), noted that:

> Successful schools are often inward looking, focussed on attainment and good management, and the survey indicates that most school leaders place the global dimension relatively low on their priorities. However, sustainable schools look outwards to engage with their local communities and have a global perspective. This wider, more inclusive vision is also seen in the strong pupil voice and involvement of pupils in decision-making ... .
>
> The emerging model of green, or sustainable, school leadership builds on what we already know about effective school leaders, but has distinct additional characteristics based on the personal values of leaders who choose to embrace sustainable development. These include fostering participation in decision making, an outward orientation looking beyond the school gates and an optimistic world view ... .
>
> These leaders are conscious of the place of the school in the local and global community ... (and) have an integrated, systemic understanding of the world and their place in it and can communicate this to others. They understand the interconnectedness of society, the environment and individuals within these contexts.
>
> (Jackson, L., 2007: 8–10)

And finally, over a three-year period Ofsted visited a sample of primary and secondary schools to see how effectively they had developed pupils' understanding of sustainability. The key findings of this research were reported in *Educating for Sustainable Development* (Ofsted, 2009), here with italics added:

- In the most successful schools, education for sustainability was an *integral element of the curriculum* and all pupils and staff contributed to improving the sustainability of their institution.
- Most of the head teachers found that, over the course of the survey, education for sustainability had been an important factor in *improving teaching and learning* more generally.
- Pupils responded particularly well to education for sustainability when it gave them the opportunity to take part in *practical activities within and outside the classroom* and enabled them

to research, plan and implement projects that made a clear difference to the school and the local community.

- A common characteristic of the lessons observed, across the full range of National Curriculum subjects seen during the survey, was the *high level of engagement* of the pupils in work they perceived as relevant to their lives and future well-being.
- The schools demonstrated how greater awareness of the need for sustainability can lead to *reduced financial costs and better management of resources* and estate.

What the extracts from these four documents provide is a snapshot of a dynamic educational response to contemporary local–global issues, a response which has been gradually developed and refined by educators over many years. This theoretical and practical expertise is invaluable in the face of the challenges that lie ahead for society. But might such ideas be contested, and if so by whom?

What is education for?

As a young teacher I certainly didn't realize that the purposes of education had been contested throughout the course of history. I just presumed that there was 'good' education and that anyone who was a trained teacher knew what that was. Perhaps this was the case when the professionalism of teachers was respected and politicians did not interfere in fields they knew little about. However, it is important to recognize that the purposes of education have long been contested. For example, which of these aims would you say was the most crucial? Should education primarily be about: *knowledge* – to pass on subject-based knowledge; *reproduction* – to ensure the continuity of societal norms; *workforce* – to create a globally competitive workforce; *religion* – to adhere to a particular religious tradition; *individual* – to bring out the best in every learner; *global* – to understand the nature of local–global interdependence; *a better world* – to help change society for the better? At different times and in different places all of these purposes have been proposed and implemented. The prioritizing of different aims always arises from different value positions. Thus there is no such thing as 'value-free' education.

Understanding the concept of ideology is vital in exploring any educational debates about values. Thus Roland Meighan and Clive Harber:

> Ideology is defined as a broad set of interlocked ideas and beliefs about the world held by a group of people that they demonstrate in both behaviour and conversation to various audiences. These

systems of belief are usually seen as 'the way things really are' by the groups holding them, and they become the taken-for-granted ways of making sense of the world.

(Meighan and Harber, 2007: 212)

In this sense one can, for example, talk about political ideologies, economic ideologies and, of course, educational ideologies. At different times and in different places some ideologies become more powerful than others: they become dominant ideologies. This may occur as a result of government diktat, military rule or state repression but it can occur in less overt ways too.

> A softer form of legitimation is in the use of major institutions, such as education, mass media, religion, law and the economy, to put over a 'consensus', 'common-sense' or 'sensible person's' point of view as against the 'lunatic fringe' view, which turns out to be almost any view inconvenient to the group with the dominant ideology.

(ibid.: 215)

The current dominant ideology in the western world is that of neoliberalism (Harvey, 2005; Gray, 2009). Among its core beliefs are the following:

- Human dignity and individual freedom are held as the central values of civilization.
- Human nature is seen as being basically competitive and thus the way in which the world works best.
- It is therefore rational for each person to maximize their own personal benefits. Economic rationality, i.e. constant competition, will bring appropriate benefits to all.
- The state should accordingly be 'weak' and not interfere with the free-market process. 'Private' enterprise is best, while 'public', i.e. state-led, initiative, is unhelpful interference
- Increased well-being will consequently occur through free trade and neoliberal globalization. However, this economic model discounts negative impacts it may have on people or environment as outside its jurisdiction.

What has been the impact of such ideas on education? Both the Conservative Party in the 1980s (under Margaret Thatcher) and Labour in the 1990s (under Tony Blair) wanted greater control of education and schools. Money spent on education became seen as wasted unless it helped the country compete efficiently and effectively in the global marketplace. A new stress on competition by results was introduced with Standard Attainment Tasks (SATs) and school league tables. The language of education now drew on market metaphors: a business model for education, parents as consumers and the notion that competition always brings out the best in learners. From then on education became based on a technocratic, managerial and performance driven view of teaching and learning (Apple, 2006). Educationalists such as Hayward (2012) have expressed concern at the degree to which both schools and society have internalized neoliberal values with their constant emphasis on competition, consumerism and individualism.

It is important to contrast this with what is sometimes referred to as 'welfare state ideology', which held sway in the UK from 1945 until well into the 1970s. Among its core beliefs are the following:

- The importance of cooperation and a sense of responsibility for the welfare of others is stressed, especially as regards the less fortunate.
- It argues that the state has a key role to play in promoting the welfare of all in society – a quite different view of society and education to that of neoliberals.
- Importantly, education is seen as a service offered by professionals (teachers) to the community – not as a commodity to be sold in the marketplace.
- Schools are also seen as having an important role to play in helping students explore both self and society. In particular, questions arise over issues of inequality and injustice in the local/global community.

Neoliberals are largely opposed to this notion of education and have strenuously opposed it, and from the 1980s onwards the neoliberal view of education has become predominant in the West.

This state of affairs has been epitomized since 2010, in the UK, by the changes implemented by the Conservative/Liberal Democratic Coalition Government, which aimed at breaking the connections between local authorities and their schools (once the norm) and the continuing opening up of education to a free market. More than half of all secondary schools are now academies rather than comprehensives and these, along with the arrival of Free schools, have dramatically altered the landscape of education (Benn, 2011; Vasagar, 2012). This is one reason why the 'high watermark' good-practice documents cited above are not quoted by the present UK government.

Even from this brief account one can see that what constitute the key purposes of education vary depending on the political parties in power. While Labour broadly supports a neoliberal view it has a more progressive view of the curriculum. How or whether education may prepare students for a future that will be very different to the circumstances of today is thus an outcome of underlying educational values and beliefs.

A long educational tradition

Over the years a wealth of educational expertise has been developed to aid educators in helping young people understand contemporary global issues and their impact on society. During the 1970s, when I was first involved in Initial Teacher Education, there was growing concern that education was failing to teach about such issues. Consequently this period saw the growth of various initiatives focusing on different aspects of the human condition. Public interest in the UN Conference on the Human Environment in 1972 prompted environmentalists and teachers to widen their focus of concern from nature conservation to exploring global environmental issues.

Similarly, NGOs (Non-Governmental Organizations) such as Oxfam and Christian Aid felt that the public were poorly informed about issues of development, i.e. global wealth and poverty, and that these issues should have a place in the curriculum. Other initiatives, such as the World Studies 8–13 Project and the Centre for Global Education, argued that a range of global issues needed to be explored in schools, from the environment, development and peace to racism, conflict and gender inequality.

During the 1980s these and other initiatives helped to make teachers and students more aware of global issues and how these impacted on their own lives and communities. Ian Lister, then Professor of Education at the University of York, welcomed these 'new movements in education', noting that:

> [their] twin stresses on human-centred education and global perspectives constitute a radical shift away from the dominant tradition of schooling (which is knowledge-centred and ethnocentric). Thus, the vanguard educators seek to give to education a new *process* and a new *perspective* on the world.
>
> (Lister, 1986: 54)

These new movements, he argued, shared eight important features – namely that:

- knowledge should have a social purpose – to ameliorate the human condition
- the curriculum should include the study of major global issues
- learning should include the learning of skills and not just content

- in order to develop such skills learning requires an action dimension
- education should be affective as well as cognitive
- the new movements recognize pluralism and diversity
- the curriculum should have a global dimension
- education should have a futures perspective.

(ibid.: 54)

This list represented both a critique of UK education in the mid-1980s and a summary of what these new movements were helping to bring to mainstream education. Over the last 25 years many of these concerns have coalesced under headings such as 'global citizenship' and 'education for sustainability' (Hicks, 2008). Much good work has been done in these fields and considerable practical expertise has been developed in teaching and learning about such matters.

More recently Think Global carried out a number of surveys that provide a valuable snapshot of the state of global learning in schools. Over three-quarters of pupils think it important to learn about how to make the world a better place but more believe global learning is important than actually receive it. 'Those who have experienced global learning ... are keen to understand more about the problems of the world, as well as being more likely than average to believe that ... people like them can make a difference' (DEA/Ipsos MORI, 2009a: 5). A companion survey on teachers' attitudes to global learning found that 94 per cent believed schools had a vital part to play in preparing school students for a fast-changing, globalized world. There was a large gap, however, between those who felt schools should do this and those who actually believed that this was realized (58 per cent). The survey felt this gap could be related to lack of confidence among teachers in developing a global perspective (DEA/Ipsos MORI, 2009b).

Self and society

One of the most succinct statements regarding what I feel education should be about came from Robin Richardson. It is this view of education that underpins the insights and initiatives described in this book:

> [We need] a synthesis between two main traditions of educational thinking ... The one tradition is concerned with learner-centred education, and the development and fulfilment of individuals. This tradition is humanistic and optimistic, and has a basic trust in the capacity and will of human beings to create healthy and empowering systems and structures. In recent years it has

been much influenced and strengthened by the new paradigms of wholeness being developed in both the physical and organic sciences, including in particular physics, biology, medicine and psychology.

The second tradition is concerned with building equality, and with resisting the trend for education merely to reflect and replicate inequalities in wider society of race, gender and class; it is broadly pessimistic in its assumption that inequalities are the norm wherever and whenever they are not consciously and strenuously resisted. Both traditions are concerned with wholeness and holistic thinking, but neither, arguably, is complete without the other. There cannot be wholeness in individuals independently of strenuous attempts to heal rifts and contradictions in wider society and in the education system. Conversely, political struggle to create wholeness in society – that is, equality and justice in dealings and relationships between social classes, between countries, between ethnic groups, between women and men – is doomed to no more than a partial success and hollow victories, at best, if it is not accompanied by, and if it does not in its turn strengthen and sustain, the search for wholeness and integration in individuals.

(Richardson, 1990: 6–7)

The guidelines referred to in this chapter represent a high water mark in official educational thinking about social and environmental responsibility. And they resonate with Richardson's view of education. The official documents endorse the thinking of many teachers and teacher educators, both primary and secondary, and create an impetus for critical and innovative thinking about the human condition. With the advent of the Conservative/Liberal Democratic Coalition Government in 2010, however, previous documentation on these matters was put aside because it did not accord with the dominant party's view of education. However, included in the government's current five aims of education are to:

- Support personal development and empowerment so that each pupil is able to develop as a healthy, balanced and self-confident individual and fulfil their educational potential.
- Promote understanding of sustainability in the stewardship of resources locally, nationally and globally.

(DFE, 2011a)

And under 'curriculum values' there is the statement: 'The curriculum should reflect values in our society that promote personal development, equality of opportunity, economic well-being, a healthy and just community, and a sustainable future' (DFE, 2011b).

One of the purposes of education therefore is *to empower young people to work towards a more sustainable future*. Schools currently have more freedom over what they teach and therefore time in which to explore these issues in greater depth. There is a wealth of expertise available on teaching about global issues and sustainability. The track record is good – but will this be enough?

Five things a school can do

- Explore the educational rationale for sustainable schools found online at www.teaching4abetterworld.co.uk/docs/download18.pdf (Chapter 5).
- Use the above source to identify appropriate opportunities in the curriculum for exploring issues of sustainability/unsustainability locally and globally.
- Consider the advantages of becoming an Eco-School (2013), i.e. part of an award programme, which can guide schools on their sustainability journey.
- Team up with supportive agencies that can give help and advice, such as Sustainability and Environmental Education (SEEd) (2013).
- Link up with other schools involved in such work locally, nationally and globally to learn from their experience.

Part One

Troubled times

Installing solar panels helps schools reduce their carbon footprint

Chapter 1

Changing climate

What is the problem?

The first rumblings about whether global warming might be taking place began in the 1980s and saw the setting up of the Intergovernmental Panel on Climate Change (IPCC) by the World Meteorological Association and the UN Environmental Programme in 1988. The role of the IPCC is not to carry out research but rather to evaluate and synthesize the research of thousands of scientists from around the world. Every few years the IPCC publishes its latest major assessment in a form aimed to help policymakers and politicians decide how to respond to climate change.

Global warming – the cause of wider climate change – is a unique man-made phenomenon, which humanity has never encountered before. Because it is a global phenomenon, it therefore presents all societies with unprecedented challenges. These include the breadth of its impact on people and environment, the length of time over which this will occur, and the actions that consequently need to be taken. The core scientific evidence from the IPCC is clear: that global warming is taking place and that it is a man-made phenomenon. Note that temperature figures given for such warming refer to the global average. Temperatures do not rise at the same rate everywhere. Some areas may actually cool down.

However, it appears that many people have flawed mental models of climate change on account of its complexity and the fact that it is an 'un-situated' risk, i.e. it is a largely invisible process, which is not directly observable. In estimating the nature and severity of possible risks, there are at least five factors that are regarded as influencing people: the cognitive, the subconscious, the affective, the socio-cultural and the individual (Helgeson *et al.* 2012). These factors highlight some of the dilemmas in raising public awareness of the need to combat climate change. While people may express concern about climate change they tend to rank it as a less important worry than the state of the economy, health care and terrorism.

A special report on climate change in the *New Scientist* (Le Page, 2011) set out what is now known to be certain and what still needs clarifying. It is known for *certain* that: emission of greenhouse gases during the twentieth century has raised the average global temperature by 0.8°C, and as a result the planet is going to get considerably hotter; that the sea level is going to rise by many metres, because when oceans warm they expand and ice melts; and that warm air holds more moisture, so there will be more floods – but in some areas also droughts. Current research is still in progress to *clarify* how high CO_2 levels may go, exactly how much hotter it will get, how quickly the sea level will rise, how different regions of the globe will be affected, and what the tipping points are that could lead to runaway global warming.

Climate change caused by global warming is beginning to affect every aspect of human life. As Mike Hulme (2009: v) observes: 'Climate change is not a "problem" waiting for a "solution". It is an environmental, cultural and political phenomenon which is reshaping the way we think about ourselves, our societies and humanity's place on Earth.'

One of the key points made in *Why We Disagree About Climate Change* (Hulme, 2009) is that it is an example of what is known as a 'wicked problem', i.e. one that defies rational or optimal solutions and at best involves 'clumsy solutions', so-called because they involve multiple voices and contradictory responses. Our children and grandchildren will live in a world that will be very different from today's as a consequence of global warming. But what if such prognostications are wrong?

As educators we've generally been brought up on the notion of 'balanced debate', i.e. that both sides of an argument should be fairly represented, and in equal proportions, in the media and in the classroom. However, while this may sometimes be so, it is often not appropriate. First, because the notion that there are only two sides to an argument (how often have I heard teachers say this) is often not the case. An argument may frequently have three or more sides to it, as anyone who has used role-play in the classroom will know. Second, because in some debates over time the scientific evidence becomes overwhelming, e.g. that smoking is harmful, and now that climate change is indeed man-made. Third, arguments about social, environmental, political and economic issues are always underpinned by the differing ideological positions that participants consciously or unconsciously hold (Goodwin, 2007).

The *Independent on Sunday* (7.2.2010) points out that:

Free-market, anti-climate change think-tanks such as the Atlas Economic Research Foundation in the US and the International Policy Network in the UK have received grants totalling hundreds of thousands of pounds from the multinational energy company ExxonMobil ... Atlas has supported more than 30 other foreign think-tanks that espouse climate change scepticism.

Note that much of the opposition to the notion of climate change comes from, and is funded by, major fossil fuel companies and organizations that espouse a free-market political ideology. It vehemently rejects environmental legislation and indeed any attempt to 'interfere' with the pursuit of financial gain. *The Guardian* (15.2.2013), for example, reports that politically conservative billionaires have secretly funded more than a hundred such groups.

These attacks came to a head in 2009, when the emails of climate scientists at the University of East Anglia were hacked in an attempt to discredit their work prior to the Copenhagen climate-change conference. But as Fred Pearce (2010) has shown in his investigations of this affair, there was nothing to disprove. Even more worrying, Naomi Oreskes and Erik Conway (2010) identified how over the years a small group of largely American scientists worked to cover up the truth about cigarette smoking and cancer, acid rain, the hole in the ozone layer, the risks of second-hand smoking and the dangers of global warming. There is therefore a long history behind the dangerous antics of climate-change sceptics and deniers. Their prime concern is not a search for scientific truth or protecting the right to be heard but instead an espousal of what might be called free-market fundamentalism, where the market is always more important than protecting the health of both people and planet (Mann, 2012).

What then is the state of our current understanding of global warming as a cause of climate change? Geographer Laurence Smith points out that we know from glacier ice, tree rings and deep ocean sediments that human activity has brought the Earth's atmosphere to a state not seen for at least 800,000 years (Smith, 2012: 24). So what are some of the possible problems ahead? Future scenarios are becoming ever more problematic. Jorgen Randers and others believe that by the mid-twenty-first century global average temperature will have increased by at least 2°C:

> There is a large body of literature about what will happen at plus 2°C. Science agrees on the broad lines – more drought in drought-prone areas, more rain in rainy areas, more extreme weather (strong winds, torrential rains, intense heat spells), more melting of glaciers and the Arctic sea ice, somewhat higher sea levels, and a more acidic ocean, in addition to the higher temperature and higher CO_2 concentration in the atmosphere.
>
> (Randers, 2012: 241)

It is the inability of governments to reach international agreement on the drastic cuts needed in greenhouse gas emissions that has led to this situation. Other studies have reported the likelihood of more rapid changes, including the thawing of Arctic permafrost, ice melt triggering natural disasters, faster rises in sea level and even greater warming (Hansen, 2011). While global warming has been slower over the last decade, global temperatures are still rising. In exploring the longer term impact of current global warming, Archer (2009) has pointed out that it might still be felt a thousand years from now, even if CO_2 emissions stopped immediately.

A recent government report on UK climate-change risks (DEFRA, 2012) identifies possible domestic impacts:

- Flooding costs could rise from the current £1.2 billion a year to £12 billion a year by the 2080s.
- Water shortages could increase, with a potential deficit of between 773 and 2,570 million litres of water a day in the River Thames.
- Farmers could experience crop losses due to flooding, and the forestry industry could see timber yield and quality reduced by drier weather.
- Rising sea levels could hit natural assets such as beaches and buildings including tourist attractions ... with knock-on impacts for businesses.
- Higher temperatures could see as many as 5,900 more people dying as a result of hot summers and heat waves by the 2050s.

Floods are now the UK's top weather threat, and the Environmental Agency has warned that Britain must become more resilient in relation to both drought and flooding (Harrabin, 2013).

Scientists now recognize that extreme weather events have become much more common, with differing emphases in different parts of the globe – bush fires in Australia, drought in the USA, snowstorms in China and flooding in the UK being recent examples (*New Scientist*, 2013). In particular it should be noted that climate change exacerbates the existing divisions between rich and poor countries, and those countries that have contributed least to global warming will suffer the greatest consequences. John Vidal (2013) observes that: 'Millions of people could become destitute in Africa and Asia as staple foods more than double in price by 2050 as a result of extreme temperatures, floods and drought that will transform the way the world farms.' It is recognized that there is a significant link between global climate change and the promotion of mental health and well-being, too. One US report expects a majority of Americans, especially children and the elderly, to suffer psychological distress from climate-related events (Coyle and Susteren, 2012), as also does an Australian study exploring the psycho-social implications of climate change (Fritze et al., 2008).

So what we are looking at here is not just more difficult weather, which we've always been good at grumbling about, but larger shifts in the climate itself. Up until recently it was argued that no *one* example of extreme weather could necessarily be attributed to climate change. However, it is now recognized that increasing extreme weather conditions – torrential rains, floods, forest fires, hurricanes and drought – are the result of climate change and are more extreme than scientists expected (*New Scientist*, 2013). Extreme is the new normal. The very meaning of what it means to live in the tropics, the arctic or the temperate regions is about to shift and dissolve in the twenty-first century into new patterns and permutations. Much that we have taken for granted for so long will be different for our children and grandchildren. How are we preparing them for this?

For one thing, most existing housing stock in the UK was not designed to cope with such changes. Inadequate standards of insulation mean that much of the heat dissipates through roof and walls, as photo-thermal imaging reveals. The sources of energy we use in buildings largely come from oil, gas and coal-fired power stations. The continued burning of such fossil fuels is one of the main contributors to global warming. Buildings are also now subject to heavier rainfall and in some places regular flooding. In the latter case costs of house insurance have gone up and some properties may even become non-insurable. We need houses that will keep us cool in times of heat and drought, where water is not wasted and where we can stay warm in cold spells.

What do you grow in your garden? Climate change will gradually alter the possibilities for the plants and vegetables that can be grown there, the insects that live there, the birds that visit. Patterns of farming will shift; some crops will disappear and new ones take their place, and patterns of land-use more widely will change. A number of tree species are already seriously threatened by insects and diseases, and this, together with climate change, will see habitats disappear along with the wildlife associated with them. Food on the supermarket shelves will differ as farming patterns change worldwide or perhaps dwindle as interruptions occur in the supply chain. Where we live, what we eat, what we wear, how we travel, what we do – all will begin to change as a result of global warming. There is no historical precedent for what lies ahead, a matter which John Urry (2011) explores in detail in *Climate Change and Society*.

What needs to be done?

As with all global issues, action on these matters needs to be taken at all levels, from international and national to regional, community and personal. The two principal tasks that need to be undertaken in response to climate change are clear: adaptation and mitigation. Adaptation requires, variously, that people learn to live with changing temperatures and seasons, higher sea levels, greater droughts, more floods and exceptional weather conditions. While the impact of these factors will vary geographically, such changes also portend changes in consumption, waste, farming, food, diet, biodiversity, land-use, buildings, travel, energy use and water use. However, for the world's poorest – those least responsible for climate change – there is little if any room for 'adaptation', a term which, Desmond Tutu (2010) argues, is fast becoming a euphemism for social injustice.

Mitigation is primarily the responsibility of the richer countries that have contributed most to global warming. It requires that every element of human behaviour that contributes to global warming be reassessed and redirected towards creation of a zero carbon society and a socially just society. Whether a lot or a little is done, individually and collectively, to adapt to and mitigate climate change, our futures and those of our grandchildren will be very different from life today since every aspect of life will need to change.

The IPCC has stressed that should average global temperatures increase by 2°C, runaway climate change may occur; hence, this is the figure below which policymakers are trying to keep. However, during the twentieth century the global average already increased by nearly 1°C. Governments, as the leading international actors, have been discussing what to do about climate change for the last twenty years. The Kyoto Protocol, which pledged to stabilize greenhouse gas emissions, was signed by nearly all nations in 1992 but did not come into force until 2005. The response of different countries to such agreements varies depending on the party in power and where the nation comes in the global poverty–wealth hierarchy. Differences between rich and poor countries about cuts in greenhouse gas emissions often lead to deadlock and the failure to agree binding targets. This is not to say that international agreements cannot be reached. But they will always be challenging because of the wide range of interests at play.

In the light of the difficulties in coordinating the stabilization of greenhouse gases internationally, national programmes become vital. All politicians and all political parties need to be constantly quizzed by the public about where they stand nationally and internationally on such agreements. However, most governments also engage in a degree of 'greenwash', implying that they are doing much more to cut emissions than they really are, as leading climate scientist James Hansen (2011) found. So, citizens must be prepared to challenge all politicians on their stance and performance in relation to global warming.

One of the most exciting publications on the need for a new energy strategy in the face of climate change is *Zero Carbon Britain 2030* (Kemp and Wexler, 2010), the second report of the Zero Carbon Britain project. This draws on ground-breaking research commissioned by the Centre for Alternative Technology and is an illuminating and authoritative display of what is possible, what is needed, and how this could be put into place if the will could be summoned.

The UK Climate Impacts Programme (UKCIP, 2013) plays a major role in working with local authorities, businesses, researchers and central government to raise awareness of the need for adaptation and for driving forward change on the ground. Its case studies illustrate how different organizations are approaching and dealing with climate-change adaptation, as, for example, in the village of Hoveringham on the River Trent: *see* Box 1.1.

Box 1.1 – Creating a resilient community flood refuge

The village of Hoveringham in Nottinghamshire is 0.5 miles from the River Trent and has a history of flooding with a 1 in 10 year flood risk. Flood alleviation work upstream has increased the future threat of flooding. Villagers had been told there was little hope of flood defences as the population does not warrant expenditure on a cost effective basis. This raised concerns locally and as a result, villagers became more interested in their own community and wanted to take action.

A flood plan was developed, with the village hall identified as a suitable place for a control centre and refuge, as it stood on higher ground. The existing village hall was not up to standard to serve as a flood refuge so it had to be upgraded. A design brief to update and enhance the space to make it suitable both as a general community facility and as a centre during flood events was developed, the work carried out and now the community has a purpose built community refuge as well as a much needed community hub.

Source: UKCIP (2013)

Climate South West (2013) is one of twelve Climate Partnerships in the UK set up to coordinate action on climate change at a local and national level. Their website states: 'Climate change is already happening now in the South West and we are already vulnerable to extreme weather. We need to plan for both current and future vulnerability.' The role of Climate South West is to raise awareness of the impacts of climate change in the south-west of England and to raise awareness of the adaptation responses that are needed. This covers all the major sectors of society from agriculture and forestry, biodiversity, business and utilities, built environment to tourism, local government, transport and health.

There are numerous examples nationally of local initiatives both to mitigate and adapt to climate change. It is sometimes said that at the personal level any changes made towards achieving a lower carbon lifestyle are not worth making. This is, of course, nonsense; for any widespread change to occur in society it needs to come from both the top down and the bottom up. Our own homes, workplaces and communities are where we first feel the impact of global warming, and there is much that can be done with immediate others in relation to mitigation and adaptation. We are each directly responsible for producing some 14 tonnes of carbon dioxide per year in Europe, through our needs for home heating, water heating, cooking, lighting, household appliances, car travel and air travel. We are also indirectly responsible for further carbon dioxide emissions when we take into account the CO_2 produced in creating the appliances we use in the house and in the production of our food. But Chris Goodall (2010) and others have set out clearly the ways in which our direct emissions can be reduced to as low as 2 tonnes of CO_2 per year. The Energy Saving Trust (2013) provides a wealth of information on every aspect of home life and shows how positive changes can be made that both save money and decrease one's carbon footprint.

These examples give a flavour of some of the attempts at climate change mitigation and adaption at different levels of society. If we do not understand what the possible responses are to dilemmas, we often turn inwards and pretend that nothing is wrong. For teachers to do this would be an educational crime.

The role of education

What role should education play in relation to the widespread and long-lasting challenges precipitated by climate change? The introduction argued that some good work in schools is going on, but that existing practice is still insufficient to prepare young people adequately for the future. The early work on children's learning and climate change was usually done by science educators, who tended to treat the issue as simply a matter of appropriate scientific knowledge. Children's understanding of global warming was often muddled and deficient, and better science teaching was seen as the remedy.

However, Fumiyo Kagawa and David Selby point out that:

At the moment, the educational response to climate change ... has tended to mirror the response of society at large ... The exhortation has been for personal change of a reformist (rather than transformative) nature. There has been ... a focus on reducing carbon emissions by the educational institution in question as well as by society at large. Climate change learning experiences have, thus, tended to be confined within 'business as usual' parameters. There has been minimal recognition of the need to engage learners in openly debating and discussing the roots, personal meanings, and societal implications of climate change scenarios that are likely to play out during their lifetimes ... The academy has tended to fiddle while Rome burns.

(Kagawa and Selby, 2010: 5)

Climate change, like many other global issues, represents a new and particularly difficult sort of problem to grapple with. If its scope, complexity and consequences make it a 'wicked' problem for scientists, politicians and the public to understand, then what does it feel like for young people? Elin Kelsey and Carly Armstrong highlight the difficulties children have when faced with messages of 'doom and gloom' in the curriculum, especially where no space is given for them to share how they feel about this:

We need to acknowledge the enormity of environmental problems, and share our feelings of frustration, anger, sadness, fear and hopelessness. We need to create spaces and opportunities to help kids explore and share their own feelings. We also need to move beyond the narrative of 'doom and gloom' toward more hopeful narratives grounded in resiliency, well-being, happiness and health.

(Kelsey and Armstong, 2012: 190)

This is not likely to happen in education unless teachers can be open to both their own, and their pupils', feelings about issues such as climate change. In a school where emotions and feelings cannot be discussed, denial and fear will always be present, if unacknowledged. Chapter 4, in particular, looks at the importance of acknowledging feelings, whether about personal or global matters, and at the ways in which this can be managed in the classroom. The evidence from work in emotional literacy is that being positively present to the emotions (the affective domain) enhances both pupil learning and behaviour.

American educator David Sobel (2008) has long argued that 'tragedies' such as climate change should not be taught about in primary school before the ages of nine or ten. What needs to come first, he argues, is developing a sense of environmental responsibility through participation in tasks such as keeping the playground tidy, growing things in the school garden and learning about recycling. He also stresses the need for younger children to become engaged with the natural world, through outside play, adventure and learning. What can be developed through such immersion in nature is biophilia, a deep love for the natural world. It is this, he argues, that provides a life foundation and source of strength that enables children to face more difficult environmental issues as they get older. This has to be an essential element in any programme of learning for sustainability

There are good materials for use in UK primary schools, for example, *Power Down: A climate change toolkit for primary schools* (Action Aid, 2009). This is designed for Key Stages 2–4 and includes a teachers' booklet with classroom ideas and photo cards showing the impact and consequences of climate change around the world. The photos are eye-catching and designed to promote pupil discussion. On the reverse side of each are key facts, discussion questions and top tips. Those relating to the UK set out ways in which schools are already saving energy and which could be implemented in the pupils' own school or home. The photos of India, Brazil and Tanzania present children facing different social and environmental consequences to those in the UK. The worksheets constantly prompt discussion and debate on each issue with questions such as: 'What do I already know?', 'What do I want to find out?', or 'What have I learned?' The toolkit also focuses on 'climate change solutions' appropriate to primary-aged children.

An interesting study by Patrick Devine-Wright *et al.* (2004) explored the issue of agency in relation to global warming, since young people seldom take action in response to it. Two groups of 9–12-year-olds were compared to see what the influence of a cooperative learning environment might be on their beliefs about global warming. The first group were members of an educational organization called the Woodcraft Folk, while the second group were non-members. The ethos of the Woodcraft Folk is of cooperation, equality, respect for the environment and interest in learning about the world. The study found that this cooperative and supportive context significantly augmented the children's understanding of issues such as global warming and their sense of agency or self-efficacy in relation to it: 'The results suggest that the conventional educational approach, typically characterized by the ethos of competition or individualistic goals and a more passive learning environment, is less successful in enabling children to develop positive beliefs about their abilities to "make a difference" in relation to serious environmental problems' (Devine-Wright *et al.*, 2004: 502). These findings raise questions about both pedagogy and child development. For example, is conventional schooling not up to the task of critical climate-change education? Can the ethos of cooperative enquiry that can be found in sustainable schools override Sobel's argument about the inappropriateness of studying such issues at primary level?

Maria Ojala (2012) identified three particular coping strategies used by Swedish 12-year-olds to deal with climate change. She defined these as problem-focused coping, de-emphasizing and meaning-focused coping. Problem-focused coping, e.g. searching for information about what one can do in the face of climate change, seems to have both negative and positive consequences. On the one hand it can lead to increased worry and anxiety. On the other hand such worry can motivate children to find information and to act on it in an environmentally efficacious way. Those who coped by de-emphasizing the seriousness of climate change were not involved in pro-environmental behaviour. Meaning-focused coping was the only strategy to have a generally positive effect. This category includes strategies such as positive reappraisal, which acknowledges the problem of climate change but then activates positive emotions in order to deal with the situation. This might be trust in scientists and technological solutions or the belief that one can engage in appropriate actions oneself to help change things. In reflecting on the implications for teachers, Ojala notes:

> While focusing on problem-focused strategies, teachers could also emphasize positive thinking, trust in different societal actors, and optimism concerning climate change, since these factors seem to shield children ... from a high degree of negative affect but also have positive relations to environmental behaviour and environmental efficacy. This does not mean that teachers should encourage naive and uncritical trust and unrealistic optimism ... It is important to help young people develop a nuanced appreciation of the complexity and dilemmas that different social actors face.
>
> (Ojala, 2012: 232)

Steven Threadgold (2012) reports that young people often exhibit 'two track thinking' in trying to make sense of the world. They are optimistic about their individual ambitions but at the same time pessimistic about the global future. Cynicism about the political process helps to contribute to their apparent feelings of powerlessness.

In the past, much of the work with older pupils simply classified climate change as a controversial issue in which the different sides of the 'debate' need balanced consideration. There might be a discussion on whether climate change was just a popular cause and thus best avoided. It might have focused on the 'controversial' nature of global warming and encouraged arguments and counter-arguments to be set out. However, while this weighing up of a contentious issue may have been appropriate some years ago, things have moved on. The academic discrediting of climate-change sceptics (referred to above) makes the notion of 'for-or-against' arguments about global warming obsolete. Geographers and others do need to debate the certain and uncertain consequences of climate change, but not the fact of its existence.

Dangers remain, however, as illustrated by a piece entitled 'Planting seeds of climate doubt':

> The political battle over whether human activity is changing earth's climate is heading for US schools. A conservative organisation is working to develop teaching materials that sow doubt on the scientific consensus over climate change, according to documents leaked ... from the Heartland Institute, a libertarian think tank based in Chicago. What's more, a separate informal poll of nearly 2000 earth science teachers suggested that a significant proportion may prove receptive to contrarian material. Nearly half of respondents reported teaching 'both sides' of climate change of their own volition. However, published peer-reviewed research does not support the existence of two equally weighted 'sides' to climate science.
>
> (Holmes, 2012: 6)

A more subtle response in England was the removal, originally, of all references to climate change and sustainability in the draft curriculum proposals for the under-14s. This caused an outcry from teachers, students and leading environmental figures (Jowitt, 2013), which led to the partial replacement of the text.

Ideas for teaching
1. Climate change: Young people's concerns
WORRYING TIMES

Both primary-school and secondary-school children express concern about global warming and climate change after watching items on the TV news, overhearing adult conversation, or being made subject to adult exhortation, peer-group myth or lessons in school. Since climate change is difficult to visualize, the implied threat can leave children with feelings that range from anxiety to resignation, to helplessness or disinterest. Generally, children are worried.

MORE INFORMATION

The knee-jerk reaction from teachers to children's worries is that young people are not in possession of enough, or of the right, information. Facts need explaining, the science needs to be made clear, the arguments weighed up, discussions and debates held. Many of the materials available do take an exploratory approach, investigating the causes and consequences of climate change and the action that pupils need to take to mitigate its impact. Although essential, this approach, on its own, is a heavy burden to bear.

HOPES AND FEARS

What children particularly need as well, as Kelsey and Armstrong (2012) point out, is a friendly and supportive space where it feels safe enough to talk about their feelings. Older children are seldom used to doing so with adults. The sharing of feelings (as against information) needs to be done in ways that respect what each individual is feeling (*see* Chapter 4). Adult and peer group acknowledgment of young people's feelings are part of an important validation process.

POSITIVE CONSEQUENCES

If this process is handled sensitively and supportively, children's fears and concerns will be shared, so they will be less acute. Learning about what other young people and adults are doing in relation to climate change lifts the spirits and can encourage personal, group and school action. Chapters 4 to 9 are all about developing a sense of personal and group agency so that one becomes, and feels, part of the solution rather than paralysed by fear and inaction over the problem.

Notes on 'Climate change – what you can do' and 'Talking with children about the environment' on the website of the Australian Psychological Society (2013) are helpful.

2. Climate change: Four dimensions of global learning

A simple but useful model, which I have used for learning about global (or local) issues, is based on the following four dimensions of learning: Knowing, Feeling, Choosing and Acting; or, in academic language, the cognitive domain, the affective domain, decision making and a sense of agency. The four basic questions for pupils and students are: What do I need to know? What do I feel about this? What choices do I want to make? What can I do myself and with others?

In this context the four categories can be further broken down as:

1. KNOWING
   - What do we think we know/need to know about climate change?
   - What are the main causes of climate change?
   - What are likely to be some of the consequences of climate change?
2. FEELING
   - What do I/we feel about climate change?
   - What are the concerns that we wish to share?
   - What are the hopes we might have?
3. CHOOSING
   - What are the options that appear to be facing us?
   - What do I/we want to see happening?
   - What should this school choose to work towards?
4. ACTING
   - What do I/we therefore need to do?
   - What are others doing: school/home/community/elsewhere?
   - Who is able to support us in what we want to do?

It should be noted that while acknowledging that children have genuine fears, I prefer the term 'concerns' as this feels more constructive in the process of capacity building.

3. Climate change: Some key elements

In terms of professional development the following provides a useful summary and overview of some of the key elements relating to climate-change education. It can be used as a template for both the planning and selection of material to suit different age groups. It is important not to approach climate change as a 'bad' thing, but rather as one of the changes in the world that we all need to understand and learn to act on.

UNDERSTANDING CLIMATE CHANGE IN THE UK
Introduction
- The main causes of climate change
- The likely consequences of climate change
- How they vary in different parts of the world

Impact on the UK
- Higher summer temperatures, and drier
- Wetter winters and more storms
- Greater coastal and river flooding

The key tasks
- How to *adapt* to these changes
- How to *mitigate* these changes

Adapting to climate change in the UK

Buildings
- Design for warmer, wetter, stormier conditions
- Check location in relation to possible flooding
- Nature and design of eco-housing
- *Key question: How and where should we build?*

Energy and water
- Reduced heating needed in winter
- Increased cooling needed in summer
- Increased water demand
- *Key question: How do we reduce energy and water consumption?*

Farming
- Longer growing season
- New crops and markets
- *Key question: How and why may farming change?*

Biodiversity
- Loss and gain of species
- Protection of species
- *Key question: What species need protecting?*

Health
- Increased incidence of some diseases, e.g. food poisoning, malaria, skin cancer
- More outdoor recreation, but exposure to sun
- *Key question: How do we stay healthy?*

Lifestyle
- Increased walking and cycling
- Increased use of urban open spaces
- Increased pressure on coast and rivers
- *Key question: How and why may our lifestyles change?*

MITIGATING CLIMATE CHANGE

Some of the main tasks of mitigation can usefully be carried out through consideration of one's own and the school's carbon footprint. All schools need to work to identify their carbon footprint and that of the local community as this is a central concept in sustainable schools (for details *see* Chapter 2), and useful information is available at Education Scotland (2013): www.ltscotland.org.uk/schoolsglobalfootprint/index.asp.

The 'eight doorways' listed in the original National Framework for Sustainable Schools identify various opportunities for both mitigation and adaptation, i.e. working towards a more sustainable future. The doorways are: Food and drink; Energy and water; Travel and traffic; Purchasing and waste; Building and grounds; Inclusion and participation; Local well-being; Global dimension. For detailed explorations and scenarios on each doorway see *Sustainable Schools, Sustainable Futures* (Hicks, 2012a).

There are thus many things that schools can do both to lessen the impact of climate change (mitigation) and to make things easier for us in the future (adaptation). In any teaching about climate change, children need to begin with opportunities to share how they feel about the issue and what they think they know. They should study existing examples of adaptation chosen from themes such as those described above and identify strategies relevant to themselves and their communities. This includes working with other pupils and staff to apply these procedures to their own school.

What is often still missing in schools, though, is a real focus on adaptation. The challenge of the key questions on adaptation can excite and engage pupils as they are presented with practical problems that relate to both school and community, and which require creative and innovative solutions. An excellent resource is *Climate Change in the Classroom* (Selby and Kagawa, 2013).

Five things a school can do

- Staff need to become knowledgeable about climate change, either through a brief presentation or a text such as *The Rough Guide to Climate Change*.
- Time needs to be set for aside for staff to share their own feelings about these matters and to discuss the implications for school policy and teaching.
- Primary schools could consider an alternative programme for younger pupils, which could develop a sense of environmental awe, wonder and responsibility.

- Every school should have a policy on mitigation and adaptation. It should be monitored and have a named member of staff to supervise its implementation.
- It is essential that the emphasis throughout is on ways in which people can adapt to change rather than confronting pupils with anxiety-producing scenarios.

Chapter 2
Easy oil

What's the problem?

Since burning fossil fuels causes climate change, every aspect of contemporary energy use has to be rethought. We not only need to face up to climate change but also to the fact that we have helped create an energy crisis. As David Buchan points out:

> Energy is what keeps us – and our way of life – going. It is something we tend to take for granted. As long as there is electricity in the wall sockets and petrol in the pumps, most of us are not worried about how the electricity is generated, or concerned about possible alternative fuel for our cars.
>
> (Buchan, 2010: vi)

While many people in the world have no connection to a power grid, a regular power supply is taken for granted in the rich industrialized nations. There may be occasional hiccups, but, like clean water, electricity is always there. However, the three main fossil fuels – coal, oil and gas – are currently the main sources of our electricity, but it is their extensive burning in the twentieth century that has led to global warming. In order to mitigate the effects of climate change the use of fossil fuels needs to be rapidly phased out and replaced by low or zero carbon energy sources. We therefore face an energy crisis, which, like global warming itself, will affect every aspect of human life. We are beginning to enter a period of energy transition that will be as profound as the shift to steam power that heralded the Industrial Revolution.

Energy is the prerequisite for all human activity, from manpower and horsepower to steam, diesel and electricity. Without energy there is no economy. Whereas the Industrial Revolution was powered by coal and the steam engine, these were gradually replaced from the early twentieth century onwards by oil. As with coal, few people had any idea of the impact the shift to oil would have on society. While use of coal and oil existed side by side for a time, by the 1960s oil was in the ascendant. Oil was a cleaner fuel, easier to transport and open to a much wider variety of uses. Not only was it used as a fuel for most forms of transport, it also played a central role in the production of fertilizers and pesticides, plastics and wide range of materials: *see* Box 2.1.

> ## Box 2.1 – Things made from oil
>
> Aspirins, sticky tape, trainer shoes, lycra socks, glue, paints, varnish, foam mattresses, carpets, nylon, polyester, CDs, DVDs, plastic bottles, contact lenses, hair gel, brushes, toothbrushes, rubber gloves, washing-up bowls, electric sockets, plugs, shoe polish, furniture wax, computers, printers, candles, bags, coats, bubble wrap, bicycle pumps, fruit juice containers, rawlplugs, credit cards, loft insulation, PVC windows, shopping bags, lipstick ... and that's just some of the things made directly from oil, not those that needed fossil fuels and the energy they consume in their manufacture (which is pretty much everything).
>
> *Source*: Hopkins, R. (2008)

Cheap oil became the golden source of energy for the twentieth century. This was taken as natural by my generation, and in geography lessons I watched with awe films showing coal and oil being wrested from the Earth in order to provide all the conveniences of modern life. It is not surprising that oil became the great addiction, given that it provides 95 per cent of transport energy and is vital to everything that we do. The consequence was that 'in the twentieth century, powerful, high-carbon, path-dependent systems were set in place, locked in through various economic and social institutions. And as the century unfolded, those lock-ins meant that the world came to be left with a high and unsustainable carbon legacy' (Elliott and Urry, 2010: 132).

Only latterly have the consequences of this bonanza been questioned. As Laurence Smith (2012: 15) explains: 'Packed inside a single barrel of oil is about the same amount of energy as would be produced from eight years of day labour by an average-sized man.' Richard Heinberg suggests that this is like having energy slaves:

> Suppose human beings were powering a generator connected to one 150-watt light bulb. It would take five people's continuous work to keep the light burning. A 100-horsepower automobile cruising down the highway does the work of 2,000 people. If we were to add together the power of all of the fuel-fed machines that we rely on to light and heat our homes, transport us, and otherwise keep us in the style to which we have become accustomed, and then compare that total with the amount of power that can be

generated by the human body, we would find that each American had the equivalent of 150 'energy slaves' working for us 24 hours each day.

(Heinberg, 2005: 30)

These benefits, so long taken for granted, are now under threat as questions have been asked about how much easily obtainable oil is left in the ground and how long it will last. It was the fossil-fuel revolution over the last century-and-a-half that led to the unprecedented period of economic growth that created all the features of modern industrial society. Given that time span it is not surprising that in recent years we mistook this extraordinary historical period to be 'normal'. It is, however, the burning of fossil fuels that has led to global warming. As Anthony Elliott and John Urry highlight, twentieth-century capitalism has created a stark contradiction.

> Its pervasive, mobile and promiscuous commodification involved utterly unprecedented levels of energy production and consumption, a high-carbon society whose dark legacy we are beginning to reap. This contradiction could result in a widespread reversal of many of the systems that constitute capitalism as it turns into its own gravedigger. A 'carbon shift' is inevitable. In the twenty-first century, capitalism seems to be unable to control those powers that it called up by the spells set in motion during the unprecedented high-carbon twentieth century, which reached its peak of global wastefulness within the neoliberal period.
>
> (Elliott and Urry, 2010: 140)

The issue of peak oil, less well known than that of climate change but inextricably related to it, has now appeared on the global agenda. In 2009 the UK Energy Research Council pointed out that 'worldwide production of oil from conventional sources could peak and go into terminal decline before 2020, and that government was not facing up to the risk' (*The Guardian*, 2009a). Voices from within the energy industry have also expressed concern:

> The world is much closer to running out of oil than official estimates admit, according to a whistleblower at the International Energy Agency who claims it has been deliberately underplaying a looming shortage for fear of triggering panic buying. The senior official claims the US has played an influential role in encouraging the watchdog to underplay the rate of decline from existing oilfields while overplaying the chances of finding new reserves.
>
> (*The Guardian*, 2009b)

An article on peak oil in *Scientific American* (2012) suggests that we have been living off an 'oil plateau' since 2005. The issue of peak oil is no longer a fringe interest and is rapidly moving centre-stage.

The notion of peak oil is best illustrated by the graph showing world oil discovery and production (*see* Figure 2.1). It shows how oil discovery peaked in the 1960s and has declined ever since. Oil production grew steadily during the twentieth century but cannot continue indefinitely, given that the major oil fields have all been discovered. While it may be possible to drill in even deeper waters or to extract oil from tar sands, the costs may be prohibitive and the environmental damage severe, as the BP Deepwater Horizon leak in the Gulf of Mexico has shown. At the same time the demand for oil keeps growing.

The term 'peak oil' refers to the intersection of these vital trends. Although it depends on who one listens to, the probability is that oil production has either peaked already, will do so in this decade or, alternatively, not for some time to come.

This matters quite simply because oil is central to every aspect of human life, from transport (road, rail, sea and air) and the production of electricity to the use of its by-products in agriculture and medicine (fertilizer, herbicides, drugs and other materials). We have allowed oil to become vital to almost everything we do. In 2010 the world consumed 87.4 million barrels of oil per day, about 32 billion barrels a year, and demand is likely to increase (Worldwatch Institute, 2012). Jeremy Leggett (2006: 22) points out that in relation to oil consumption, 'society is in a state of collective denial that has no precedent in history, in terms of its scale and implication'.

What we are actually faced with is not the end of oil but the end of 'easy' oil. While new oil finds are occurring they are too small to make up for the speed at which the major fields are depleting. Although non-conventional oils, such as the Canadian tar sands, could help meet global demand, the amount of energy, water, money and environmental damage needed to extract them could make extraction prohibitive (Strahan, 2012). Similar serious objections apply to the hydraulic fracturing – 'fracking' – of shale rocks to obtain natural gas (Rawnsley, 2012; Brooks, 2013). Whichever way one looks at the issue, energy prices are likely to rise as demand for oil outstrips supply. Radical social and political changes will be needed to meet the challenges of a post-oil world.

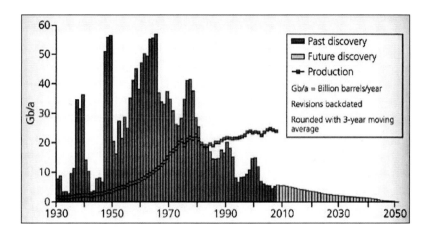

Figure 2.1: The dilemma of peak oil

ASPO Newsletter (2008)

In the same way that the issue of climate change has been met by scepticism and denial, so has the notion of peak oil. The difference, however, is that while the scientific community is very largely agreed on the existence of man-made climate change, energy experts, including the big oil companies themselves, are as yet divided over the issue of peak oil (Bridge and Wood, 2010). There are many reasons why people might prefer to ignore the possibility or likelihood that oil has peaked. First, it would demand such a widespread change to rich-world lifestyles that it is barely conceivable after a century of cheap oil. Second, even if one contemplates its possibility, it is easier to deny its likelihood than face up to the consequences. Third, there are too many vested interests, from the oil extraction industry itself to energy suppliers and the global agribusiness corporations. Fourth, it threatens the dominant ideology of free-market economics, which claims the freedom to act as it will in the pursuit of profits (Urry, 2013).

Thus, says Richard Heinberg (2007: 19), 'a conclusion of startling plainness presents itself: *our central survival task for the years ahead, as individuals and as a species, must be to make a transition away from the use of fossil fuels – and to do this as peacefully, equitably, and intelligently as possible*' (italics in the original).

What needs to be done?
It is first important to note that many critics, some of whom once worked in the oil industry, are well aware that a business-as-usual scenario for the future is impossible and are arguing for a rapid move towards renewable energy sources and a zero-carbon society (ASPO International, 2013; The Oil

Drum, 2013; Kemp and Wexler, 2010). The US military has warned that there could be serious oil shortages by 2015 (Macalister, 2010). A significant and important response from business has been the setting up of the UK Industry Taskforce on Peak Oil and Energy Security, which published *The Oil Crunch: A wake-up call for the UK economy* (ITPOES, 2010).

Historically, the transition from one energy source to another involves a long and expensive transition, because of the enormous capital invested in the production, transport, refining and use of oil and all the paraphernalia that goes with it. To phase out petrol-driven vehicles, service stations and pumps and to introduce electric vehicles, charging stations and new electric grids, for example, would take several decades. As Martenson (2011: 163) comments, 'The only way to conceivably avoid this delay would be to override the markets and force the transition by government decree.'

Thus it appears that a variety of fuels will be in use over the next several decades. Coal is by far the dominant energy source for the production of electricity, and its use has been growing to its highest global consumption since the 1960s. This puts climate change targets seriously at risk. While the nuclear option is hailed as a zero carbon energy source, ways of storing its highly dangerous waste far into the future have yet to be resolved. In the UK Cumbria has rejected proposals for the storage of nuclear waste, and management at the Sellafield nuclear waste reprocessing plant has been lambasted by MPs (Macalister, 2013). Natural gas could provide a 'bridge fuel' in the transition, because converting vehicles to run on gas is a lot easier than starting from scratch with electric vehicles.

The long-term emphasis has to be on renewable sources of energy, including solar photovoltaic cells, solar thermal technology, wind power, tidal and wave power, micro-hydropower, biomass (i.e. energy for heating derived from plant material, vegetation or agricultural waste) and combined heat and power plants. Renewables are actually the fastest growing power source. This transformation in turn will require significant changes to the national electricity grid as power sources will be located over a much wider area than present power stations.

Currently 87 per cent of world energy use is made up of coal, oil and gas, 5 per cent is from nuclear energy and 8 per cent from renewable sources. While the availability of easy oil will begin to decline in the future, oil that is more difficult and expensive to obtain will probably be drilled to the last drop because of the demand for it. The intermediate solution is likely to be an increase in the use of coal, which itself will be replaced by gas, since this produces two-thirds lower carbon emissions. The eventual real winners by mid-century need to be solar, wind and biomass. Overall therefore, carbon emissions will continue to increase unless all the remaining fossil fuels are left in the ground, and it is this reality that needs to be our starting point (Berners-Lee and Clark, 2013).

Four areas of focus that can serve to illustrate the work being done towards a post-carbon world are buildings, transport, food and renewable energy.

Buildings

Buildings are responsible for both energy demand and carbon emissions, and most people have some responsibility for a building, be it a home or workplace. The first obvious steps are to consider how energy use in the building can be reduced. The means include improving the insulation, blocking draughts, turning thermostats down and heating only the rooms that are actually being used. Energy bills will come down and emissions will reduce. A more extensive programme occurs with building refurbishment aimed at low- or zero carbon standards. One exemplar scheme in South Wales, initiated by the Heads of the Valley Strategic Regeneration Programme, aims to make Aberdare the UK's first low-carbon town. This is a 15-year project funded by the Welsh Assembly Government. It aimed to refurbish 8,500 homes by 2014 and convert 8 schools to solar power. Energy performance checks ensure properties are given suitable energy saving advice. The initiative includes low-energy street lights, solar thermal hot-water heating systems, smart meters, solar photovoltaic panels and air-source heat pumps. Residents say that their fuel bills have been cut in half (Lean, 2011).

Interest is also growing in new-build sustainable housing, where the buildings have been designed from the start as low or zero carbon. The Green Building Store in Denby Dale, West Yorkshire, has taken the well-known German Passivhaus model and adapted it for the UK market (Click Green, 2010). The house uses 90 per cent less energy for heating compared with a standard home, and heating costs should be around £70 per year. This is because it is twenty times more airtight than a normal house and remarkably well insulated. Because of this it does not need solar panels to produce electricity for heating. An excellent source of information on low carbon living, with inspiring case studies, is Chris Bird's (2010) *Local Sustainable Homes*, which covers both the retrofitting of existing properties and the creation of new eco-villages.

Transport

It has long been taken for granted that everyone should have the right to travel where they like, when they like, as fast as they can and in whatever form of transport they choose. The result is huge traffic flows within towns and between them, particularly in industrialized and urbanized countries. Car owners and road hauliers complain about rises in the cost of fuel, but many would complain even more loudly about any infringement on the right to infinitely roam. However, given the combination of climate change and peak oil, such freedom is unsustainable: a transport paradigm shift is needed in order to create a zero carbon future.

Elements of this sustainable transport paradigm are already visible around the world, often summed up in the slogan 'Avoid, Shift, Improve'. *Avoidance* is about limiting unnecessary journeys by road, through congestion charging and changing to more sustainable forms of transport. *Shifts* to more sustainable forms of travel can be seen in bus rapid transport systems, pedestrianization, cycle ways and rail-based mass transit systems. *Improved* vehicle efficiency is occurring through stricter fuel efficiency regulations, electric bikes and high-efficiency cars and trucks (Replogle and Hughes, 2012).

Most of the principal vehicle manufacturers now have an interest in the design and testing of electric cars – vehicles with an electric motor powered by an on-board battery, which can be recharged via electrical sockets, including designated recharging points in the public places of some cities. Current models are at the expensive end of the market, but it is anticipated that prices will come down as this initiative grows in scope. The movement towards electric cars has been specifically driven by concern about oil prices, dependence on foreign oil, and by the need to reduce greenhouse gas emissions. The range a car can travel on one battery charge is steadily increasing as design improves. But such developments also require changes in local and national infrastructure. In north-east England, for example, over sixty partners, ranging from local authorities and small businesses to retailers and transport providers, have signed up to the Plugged in Place project, which aims to offer 1,000 charging points by 2013 (Next Green Car, 2012). It should be noted that for electric vehicles to be *really* carbon-free, their electricity needs to come from renewable sources rather than oil- or coal-fired sources. In a post-carbon society it is also likely that fewer journeys will be made as life becomes more localized in a sustainable future. Certainly, the present car system will have been replaced (Dennis and Urry, 2009).

Food and farming

While food and farming will be significantly influenced by issues relating to peak oil, less seems to be written about this issue, despite the fact that it is due to become another emerging dilemma. Modern industrialized agriculture is heavily dependent on oil and oil-based products, using fertilizers to increase yield and pesticides to control biological threats, as well as fuel to operate farms and transport food across the globe. There has been a growing realization that food issues could become more difficult in the future, and a few years ago, for the first time since the Second World War, the Labour Government planned a twenty-year food and farming strategy, which would have integrated food policy across every government department to be coordinated by the Department for Environment, Food and Rural Affairs (DEFRA):

> It acknowledges formally for the first time ... that the UK's food production and distribution affects not just the countryside and environment but our health, social equity, and whether we will even have enough to eat, as natural resources dwindle and climate change disrupts farming. It also recognises the fragility of the current UK food system, which depends heavily on imports, last-minute ordering, and long distribution chains, which are vulnerable to sudden shocks from global price spikes, disruption to food supplies, and the impact of climate change on critical infrastructure, such as ports.
>
> (Lawrence, 2010)

Earlier studies, for example from the Policy Foresight Institute (2008) and the Soil Association (2008), raised questions about whether Britain ought to be able to feed itself and whether our food system was as secure and resilient as it needed to be. The Soil Association pointed to the vulnerability of UK and EU food and farming systems to climate change and to the way in which scarcer, costlier oil is underplayed in current policy; the Association also called for incentives to encourage low carbon farming. Tim Lang (Lang and Heasman, 2004), a leading expert on agriculture and food policy, has long stressed a future clash between three differing paradigms of food and farming: the gigantic industrialized model, based on high carbon inputs, developed in the twentieth century; the biotechnology model, based on genetic manipulation and modification of crops; and the ecological model, based on holistic and organic approaches to farming. Our food future may well be marked by competition between biotech and organic visions of food and farming in different markets and geographical areas. Only organic methods encourage a low-carbon form of agriculture.

One of the key features of organic farming is that food would be healthier and more locally produced. Tamzin Pinkerton and Rob Hopkins in *Local Food* (2009: cover) provide a compendium of hands-on case studies of what this looks like in action.

Many people already buy their vegetables as locally as possible, eat organic and seasonal food when they can, and may even be getting to grips with managing an allotment. But with current economic pressures and mounting concerns about climate change and peak oil, there is a growing feeling that we need to do more to reduce dependence on the global food market.

The authors discuss home gardens, allotments, community gardens, community orchards, farmers' markets, food cooperatives, local food guides and events, and show how the shift to a low carbon form of farming is already beginning.

Renewable energy

The most visible response to peak oil is the burgeoning interest in renewable energy, although generally it is in terms of a reaction to climate change. Investment in renewables is occurring primarily as a way of cutting greenhouse gas emissions caused by fossil fuels. The fact that peak oil is going to cause another whole raft of issues is secondary in terms of public awareness. Leggett (2006) and others have stressed the need for a 'big portfolio' approach to the retreat from oil, pointing out that no one technology can provide the country's energy demand but that a mix-and-match approach is needed from the family of renewable technologies: *see* Box 2.2. House owners are increasingly installing solar panels to cut both carbon emissions and electricity bills.

BOX 2.2 – MAIN SOURCES OF RENEWABLE ENERGY

SOLAR
- Solar photovoltaic (PV) panels on roofs and at ground level
- Solar thermal both water heating and electricity production

WATER
- The use of tidal and wave power to generate electricity
- Micro-hydropower based on turbines in streams and rivers

WIND
- On-shore wind farm turbines in appropriate areas
- Off-shore wind farm turbines at sea, local and deep water

BIOMASS
- Burning waste products from farming and forestry
- Burning energy crops and processed fuels such as wood pellets

---

CHP
- Local schemes providing Combined Heat and Power
- Higher efficiency than when just generating electricity

Source: Hicks (2012a)

So after 'easy oil' comes 'difficult oil' and this is the phase we are now entering. It's not clear how long this continuing phase of fossil fuel use will last, but it will eventually have to give way to low carbon sources as renewables become more important. However, at the time of writing the UK's Coalition Government was not unanimous in its support of renewables, believing that the final decision should be left to free-market economics (Carrington, 2012). Since it was the market that helped create the current crisis, this does not bode well for the future. What is needed is clear and unambiguous zero-carbon directives and leadership from a government, otherwise this leaves the biggest and most urgently needed energy shift in history to chance.

The role of education

It still seems relatively rare to find work going on in UK schools that directly refers to peak oil. This is probably for several reasons: because, after a century of cheap oil, running out of oil is a barely comprehensible idea; because it is easier to deny than face up to the consequences; and because the belief persists that new technology will always sort things out. If this is currently the public perception (or lack of perception), then it is also likely to be reflected in mainstream education. An internet search of one major geography education website for references to peak oil, for example, only came up with 'Peak District'.

This does not mean that good work is not going on in schools. As part of sustainability education, children often explore issues to do with saving energy, carbon footprints and the importance of renewable sources of energy. This work has largely arisen out of awareness that education has an important role to play in the future reduction of carbon emissions as part of climate change mitigation. Children are thus increasingly aware of the need to conserve energy, both at home and at school, and to learn more about renewable sources of energy. I do not think that pupils need to learn about peak oil *per se* at primary level, but that they do need to learn about where their energy comes from, how it has been generated and why it should not be wasted. They could be learning about the advantages and disadvantages of different energy sources, but this should not be presented as a difficulty or a problem, lest it cause worry and alarm. Neither should it be about 'bad' sources (fossil fuels) and 'good' sources' (renewables). It should be done as an exciting story about change, in this case changes in the way we create our energy. Focusing on actual examples of renewable technologies in action can lead to a sense of agency and positive engagement with energy issues.

Ideas for teaching

1. Rethinking energy: Four dimensions of global learning

A simple but useful model, which I have used for learning about global (or local) issues, is based on the following four dimensions of learning: Knowing, Feeling, Choosing and Acting; or, in academic language, the cognitive domain, the affective domain, decision making and a sense of agency. The four basic questions for pupils and students are: What do I need to know? What do I feel about this? What choices do I want to make? What can I do myself and with others?

In this context the four categories can be further broken down as:

1. KNOWING
   - What do we think we know/need to know about our uses of energy?
   - What are the main sources of energy used in society today?
   - What are the consequences of using these different forms of energy?
2. FEELING
   - What do I/we feel about our uses of energy today?
   - What are the concerns we may wish to share?
   - What are the hopes we might have?
3. CHOOSING
   - What are the energy options that appear to be facing us?
   - What changes do I/we want to see happening in relation to energy?
   - What energy options should this school work towards?
4. ACTING
   - What do I/we therefore need to do?
   - What are others doing: school/home/community/elsewhere?
   - Who is able to support us in what we want to do?

2. Rethinking energy: Some key elements

In terms of professional development the following offers a summary of some of the key elements relating to energy use today. It can be used as a template for both the planning and selection of material to suit different age groups. An excellent resource is *The Rough Guide to the Energy Crisis* (Buchan, 2010).

Introduction
- The multiple uses of energy in daily life
- How much we use and how much we waste
- The burning of fossil fuels creates global warming

Fossil fuels
- The abundance of coal and its carbon footprint
- The end of easy oil and its carbon footprint
- Natural gas and its smaller carbon footprint
- Nuclear energy: no carbon footprint but dangerous waste

Renewable sources
- Wind farms on land and off-shore
- Solar power on roofs and in open spaces
- Water power from rivers and tides
- Biomass, burning wood, farm waste and plants

A post-carbon future
- A transition from fossil fuels to renewable sources
- Learning to use, and live with, less energy
- The widespread take-up of zero-carbon sources
- The manner in which all aspects of life will need to change

3. A lesson on peak oil

Box 2.3 highlights several ways in which one might begin to explore issues relating to peak oil with older pupils. It is done in a way that catches the imagination and provokes discussion and debate, while presenting the issue as a challenge to engage with rather than as a threat to fear. The fact that the school concerned could call on the resources of its local Transition group was a bonus but all schools can make such links (*see* Chapter 6) via the Transition Network (2013).

BOX 2.3 – LIFE BEYOND OIL

This is a summary of a lesson with Year 9 students (13–14)

INTRODUCTION

Produce a large bag containing all kinds of household objects – trainers, hair gel, cycle inner tubes, spoons, and so on – and ask the students what all these things have in common. Let the suggestions fly for a while until you have unpacked the whole bag, and then, if no-one has got it, tell them that they are all made from by-products of oil. Then produce a litre bottle of oil, and make the point that a couple of tablespoons of it contain more energy than they could exert in a day, and that their lives require the equivalent of 50 people in their back garden pedalling frantically on bikes day and night. Then split them into five groups, each group on a separate table with a different exercise on it. Move them round to another table every 15 minutes.

ACTIVITIES

1. The journey

Where does oil come from and what does peak oil mean in practice? What kind of state is the supply we depend on in? For this exercise you'll need a computer online, logged onto David Strahan's Oil Depletion Map (www.davidstrahan.com/map.html), and to have given each group a sheet which asks them six questions* they can only find answers to by roving around the map. This gives a good background and gets them thinking about what peak oil means and in particular how vulnerable the UK is becoming.

2. War and oil

On this table, divide the group into two teams, and invite them to debate the motion 'The Iraq War (2003–2011) was caused by oil'. Cards with various possible reasons for the war, such as 'WMD' (Weapons of Mass Destruction), 'oil', 'democracy' and so on can be arranged on the table, and the students invited to rank them in order of importance as they see them.

3. What you can do with oil

On the table with the contents of your bag of oil-made items place a card reading: 'Oil can be used to make a vast array of plastics, glues, paints, varnishes, medicines and other materials, most of which we take for granted in our lives. On this table are many things that we looked at earlier. Your task for the next ten minutes is to find at least one thing in this room that is not made using oil. If you can't do that, try to think of something at home. You will need to think about all the elements and components of the objects you are thinking of.' The group we did this with came up with three things, which were: 'Ourselves, hair, and the water in that jug'.

4. How is oil used

On this table place a pile of copies of the local newspaper and some red marker pens, as well as some photocopies of the same paper from the 1930s and 1940s (some rummaging around online, in the local library or museum, should provide these). In pairs, ask the students to go through the papers and circle any article which involves the use of oil, including adverts. Using the 1940s cuttings offers an insight back to a time when the pressure was to use less, not more oil, and the contrast between the Second World War and today can be quite illuminating.

5. Life beyond oil

The card on this table reads 'Whether we see life beyond oil as a threat or an opportunity will be down to us. Do we choose to see the move away from oil dependence as a disaster, or an opportunity to build something better?' Prepare sheets of flip-chart with two columns, 'What would you look forward to?' and 'What would you miss?' and invite the students to brainstorm things for each column.

*Oil depletion questions: 1. Finland, Sweden and Greenland don't export oil. Why not? 2. Which country produced more oil in 2010: China, India or Saudi Arabia? 3. In which year did the United States peak in production? 4. UK oil and gas production peaked in 1999. We increasingly rely on gas from Norway and Russia. Why might this not be such a good idea? 5. Which of the following countries has the most promising long-term supply – Kuwait, Iran, Iraq or Syria? 6. Countries such as China and Venezuela are increasingly standing up to the United States. What do you think might make them feel able to do so?

Source: Hopkins, R. (2008)

4. The Ashden Awards

The Ashden Awards for sustainable energy are given each year to outstanding initiatives around the world, including schools, which demonstrate the use of renewable energy. The award website is full of exciting initiatives to whet the appetite and prompt reflection on what one's own school might be able to achieve.

While these are accounts of a prize-winning school it should be remembered that all such initiatives have small beginnings, perhaps with pupils just investigating where the school's energy comes from. The Ashden Awards (2013) website is inspiring.

Five things a school can do

- Staff need to become knowledgeable about energy issues in school via the Ashden Awards website: www.ashden.org/schools.
- Time needs to be set aside for staff to share their own feelings about these matters and to discuss the implications for school policy and teaching.
- Every school should have its own policy document on energy-saving, and this should be monitored and have a named person to supervise its implementation.
- Awareness of these matters should be introduced into curriculum and practice in such a way that they become the norm for both children and teachers.
- It is essential that the emphasis throughout is on how people can adapt positively to change rather than confronting pupils with anxiety-producing scenarios.

Chapter 3

Growing limits

What's the problem?

Forty years ago *The Limits to Growth* (Meadows *et al.*, 1972) triggered a global debate that is even more crucial and relevant today. It attracted global headlines at the time because, well before the days of the personal computer, it was the first computer simulation to explore the possible future impact of global trends. The five trends studied then were: accelerating industrialization, rising population growth, widespread malnutrition, depletion of non-renewable resources and environmental damage. Although some predictions were challenged, the broad thrust of the book, which emphasized how these trends might interact, was revolutionary in challenging the modern obsession with growth (MacKenzie, 2012).

Much of the subsequent criticism came from those who believed technology and resource economics would always overcome any possible ecological limits to growth. Ugo Bardi (2011: 94) points out in his retrospective on *Limits to Growth* that: 'Misunderstanding was enhanced by a media campaign very similar to the one that has been recently directed against climate science'. Bardi argued that this therefore set further work on global modelling back by decades. I still have a faded photocopy of the front page of *The Observer*, of 27 June 1971, which read: 'Shock findings on the environment crisis – the more we try the worse it will be'. For many like me, the book was a wake-up call, because however each trend was changed the resulting scenarios saw unchecked growth leading to overshoot and collapse in the twenty-first century. In updated work, the authors used more powerful computer modelling to confirm the need for society to move rapidly towards a more sustainable path (Meadows *et al.*, 2005). One of the original authors has completed a new follow-up study, mentioned later.

Part of the problem in all this lies in the conflicting views of economists and ecologists. Economists tend to believe that there are no limits to growth, whereas ecologists recognize the finiteness of the Earth's natural systems, in terms of both how much can be taken from them and how much waste they can absorb. Gardner and Prugh point out that:

> The world is very different, physically and philosophically, from the
> one that Adam Smith, David Ricardo, and other early economists

knew – different in ways that make key features of conventional economics dysfunctional for the twenty-first century ... In Smith and Ricardo's time nature was perceived as a huge and seemingly inexhaustible resource: global population was roughly 1 billion – one seventh the size of today's – and extractive and production technologies were far less powerful and invasive.

(Gardner and Prugh, 2008: 4)

Most economists would nevertheless still argue that what will save the world is continued economic growth. Yet world fisheries are on the verge of collapse, oil production may have already peaked and climate change continues to bring new hazards. The assumption that economic activity is somehow independent from nature no longer holds true. Ecologists and others have long argued that technological solutions on their own will not bring about a sustainable society; that exponential growth can lead to sudden catastrophes, both economic and environmental; and that problems cannot be dealt with in isolation but only when seen as part of an organic whole. Taking the biosphere as its model, the UN Biodiversity Report insists that there are definite limits to growth and that we urgently need to learn to live within these limits (*The Guardian*, 2010).

One way of measuring human impact on the planet is through a tool called the Ecological Footprint, developed by the New Economics Foundation and the Global Footprint Network in 2012. This considers all the natural resources that we take from the planet and all the consequent waste that we put back into the biosphere. For our planetary life-support system to function effectively, our collective footprint needs to match what the restorative systems of the planet can handle. If resources are turned into waste more quickly than waste can be turned back into resources, global ecological overshoot occurs.

Throughout most of history, humanity has used nature's resources – to build cities and roads, to provide food and create products, to absorb the CO_2 generated by human activities – at a rate well within the means of what the Earth could regenerate. But sometime in the mid-1970s (just after publication of *Limits to Growth*), we crossed a critical threshold. Human demand began outstripping what the planet could renewably produce, a gap known as ecological overshoot:

According to our calculations, we are now using the Earth's resources at a rate that would take between 1.3 and 1.5 planets to sustainably support. The research shows us on track to require the resources of two Earth's well before mid-century. The fact that we are using, or 'spending', natural capital faster than it can replenish is similar to having expenditures that continually exceed income. In planetary terms, the costs of our ecological overspending are becoming more clear by the day. Climate change – a result of carbon being emitted faster than it can be reabsorbed by the forests and oceans – is the most obvious and arguably pressing result. But there are others – shrinking forests, species loss, fisheries collapse and freshwater stress to name but a few. The environmental crises we are experiencing are symptoms of looming catastrophe. Humanity is simply using more than the planet can provide.

(Global Footprint Network, 2013)

A graphic illustration of this is the concept of Earth Overshoot Day – that is, the approximate date each year on which human demands exceed the planet's ability to replenish. In 2011 this fell on September 27. The deficit is made up by unsustainable depletion of fisheries, forests and minerals and CO_2 emissions. In 2012 overshoot day was August 22.

In terms of human history something changed forever in the late twentieth century. This was the notion that there would always be growth, because that is what 'progress' is all about, but also the realization that our growing global ecological footprint had led to overshoot. These were mutually incompatible trends, the former causing the latter. Current forms of growth must end – will end – because they are threatening the planet's life support systems. 'This is not a temporary condition; it is essentially permanent,' says Richard Heinberg (2011: 2). The temptation is always to take one aspect of environmental or social damage and presume that if this can be resolved things will 'go back to normal'. But the different aspects are symptoms of the larger disequilibrium that has been created in the global system by human excess.

Chris Martenson (2011) highlights two distinct forms of growth. In the case of linear growth, something increases by the same amount each time, as in the number sequence 1,2,3,4,5,6,7. Geometric or exponential growth, however, is marked by a doubling in the amount each time, as in the sequence 1,2,4,8,16,32,64. Much of the growth that has occurred in the twentieth century, such as in the world's population, has been exponential. In Martenson's words (2011: 29), 'Speeding up is a critical feature of exponential growth – things just go faster and faster, especially towards the end'. Since we are surrounded by examples of exponential growth, he asserts, it is important to remember three vital concepts: i) *Speeding up*: time gets compressed towards the end of exponential growth; ii) *Turning the corner*: in systems that have limits, this is the danger point; iii) *More than double:* each doubling is more than all the previous doublings combined. World population growth, use of fossil fuels, greenhouse gas emissions have all been growing exponentially. Like the great oil super-tankers at sea, they take a long time to slow down and stop, so that:

> the scale of our collective impact on the planet has grown to such an extent that many scientists contend that Earth has entered a new geologic era – the *Anthropocene*. Humanly generated threats to the environment's ability to support civilization are now capable of overwhelming civilization's ability to adapt and regroup.
>
> (Heinberg, 2011: 145)

Lest the limits-to-growth argument is thought to be somewhat *passé*, we need to reflect on a global forecast for the next forty years compiled by Jorgen Randers (2012), one of the authors of the original *Limits to Growth* report. His work is based on extensive and detailed analysis of all the relevant global trends and it confirms that there is a rocky road ahead. He chose to look forward forty years because it was forty years since the first *Limits to Growth* report came out. He focuses particularly on population and consumption, energy and CO_2, food and carbon footprint, in order to establish five regional futures that could well occur by 2052. He writes:

> The transition to sustainability will require fundamental change to a number of the systems that govern current world developments. Not only will the energy system need to change from fossil to solar, and the ruling paradigm from perpetual physical growth to some form of stability that fits within the physical carrying capacity of the globe, but there will also be changes to the softer institutional guides like capitalism, democracy, agreed power sharing, and the human perspective on nature.
>
> (Randers, 2012: 13)

When systems are in ecological overshoot, says Randers, there are only ever two ways out – collapse or managed decline. The next forty years matter because they are about beginning to manage that decline. Clearly there will be tensions and strife.

In the twenty-first century we are facing a period of unprecedented change and consequent turbulence, marked by rampant consumerism in the rich world and an increasing loss of direction. As Tony Judt observes:

Something is profoundly wrong with the way we live today. For thirty years we have made a virtue out of the pursuit of material self-interest: indeed, this very purpose now constitutes whatever remains of our sense of collective purpose. We know what things cost but have no idea what they are worth ... The materialistic and selfish quality of contemporary life is not inherent in the human condition. Much of what appears 'natural' today dates from the 1980s: the obsession with wealth creation, the cult of privatization and the private sector, the growing disparities of rich and poor. And above all, the rhetoric which accompanies these: uncritical admiration for unfettered markets, disdain for the public sector, the delusion of endless growth.

(Judt, 2010: 1–2)

The current global economic recession bears witness to the effects of such unbridled growth and greed in a financial world driven by free-market capitalism. John Gray writes:

The type of globalisation that has been in place over the last twenty years is undergoing an irreversible collapse. The global free-market was stable only on the assumption that it could be self-regulating; but when economies are so closely interwoven the entire system becomes dangerously fragile ... An integrated system is prone to break down when any of its parts ceases to function, and this what began to happen when the American sub-prime mortgage crisis struck America in 2007.

(Gray, 2009: xiv)

He continues:

Global laissez-faire rested on the belief that the market is in some sense fundamentally rational. The assumption was that players in the market could use a version of scientific method in making their bets, so that any disequilibrium in the system would be self-correcting. But this was taking a narrow conception of rationality to an unreasonable extreme.

(Gray, 2009: xv)

Gray (2009), Harvey (2005) and Judt (2010) document in detail the ways in which such neoliberal practices, while historically designed to improve human well-being, at the same time cause 'creative destruction' – in the division of labour, in social relations, in welfare provision, in technological development and in attachment to the land. Other recent critiques of the need for constant growth have focused on 'turbo-consumerism' (Lawson, 2009), the destruction of habitat and community (McKibben, 2007) and the need for more sustainable economies (Worldwatch Institute, 2010).

What needs to be done?

All the hazards described so far are, at heart, about the 'limits to growth' and this has led to countless initiatives around the globe focusing on the need to create more sustainable futures. Whether at intergovernmental, governmental, NGO, regional, local or personal level, all are working to change aspects of unsustainable practice to more sustainable modes, often with significant success (Visser, 2009a, 2009b). To create a more sustainable future requires change from both bottom up and top down. Box 3.1 is a brief reminder of different aspects of unsustainable practice that are being tackled worldwide in different ways.

> ### Box 3.1 – Aspects of a post-carbon society
>
> #### Energy
> Continued reliance on fossil fuels is helping cause major climatic change, while nuclear power is increasingly a social, economic and environmental liability. A post-carbon future will emphasize greatly increased energy efficiency and the use of renewable energy resources such as solar, wind, water.
>
> #### Transport
> Unrestricted use of the car has created a major series of related problems, from severe traffic congestion and dangerous air pollution to urban sprawl. A post-carbon future will minimize the need for people to travel, with jobs closer to home, and emphasize the use of public transport (including buses and trams) and cycling.
>
> #### Environment
> Unrestrained consumption of the earth's resources is producing irreversible damage to the biosphere and a major loss of biodiversity. In a zero-carbon future people will see themselves as a part of the natural world rather than as separate from it, and environmental quality will be as important as economic well-being.

ECONOMICS

Traditional models of development focus narrowly on economic growth as the indicator of 'progress'. Various costs are 'discounted', e.g. environmental damage, impact on the poor, effect on future generations. A post-carbon society will use more comprehensive indicators of well-being based on green principles.

CITIES

Uncontrollable urban growth is having a profound impact on human/planetary well-being in the rich and poor world alike. In a post-carbon future, planning will be more participatory and land-use and transport policies carefully integrated. Homes, jobs, services, amenities will be mixed together and thus more easily accessible.

POVERTY

Debt and falling export prices encourage unsustainable development in much of the world. A post-carbon future for all requires a major change of direction in the policies and lifestyles of the Northern hemisphere and increased international support for greater equity and justice.

RESOURCES

In a post-carbon future, waste reduction will replace rubbish disposal. Planned obsolescence, convenience, and the throwaway society will be seen as aberrations. Manufacturing will become less energy-intensive and less polluting. More items will be reused, recycled or burnt to extract energy.

FARMING

Current intensive farming often leads to extensive land degradation and a massive effort is needed to protect soil and conserve water. In a post-carbon future there will be more emphasis on organic husbandry and mixed farming with biological pest controls. More food will be grown and consumed locally and regionally.

Meadows *et al.* (2005) argue that a sustainable society cannot be fully realized until it can be widely imagined and envisioned. This is why education for sustainability has a crucial role in helping each generation visualize the sort of changes that need to come about (*see* Chapter 9). As a way of encouraging this process, they list some of the things that they feel would be vital in a more sustainable society.

- Leaders who are honest, respectful, intelligent, humble, and more interested in doing their jobs than in keeping their jobs, more interested in serving society than winning elections.
- An economy that is a means, not an end one that serves the welfare of the environment, rather than vice versa.
- Regenerative agriculture that builds soils, uses natural mechanisms to restore nutrients and controls pests, and produces abundant, uncontaminated food.
- The preservation of ecosystems in their variety, with human cultures living in harmony with those ecosystems; therefore, high diversity of both nature and culture.
- Reasons for living and for thinking well of ourselves that do not involve the accumulation of material things

(Meadows *et al.*, 2005: 273–4)

The traditional tools for measuring the state of a nation's 'health', such as GNP (Gross National Product) or GDP (Gross Domestic Product), are clearly no longer adequate as they focus narrowly on economic output. There has thus been interest for some time in establishing a new form of economics (Boyle and Simms, 2009) and alternative indicators of well-being, notably the Happy Planet Index. It measures 'the extent to which countries deliver long, happy, sustainable lives for the people that live in them according to global data on life expectancy, experienced well-being and ecological footprint (New Economics Foundation, 2013).

Tim Jackson, in *Prosperity Without Growth: Economics for a finite planet* (2009), points out that the financial crash and subsequent global recession did not arise from casual oversight or individual greed: 'The economic crisis is not a consequence of isolated malpractice in selected parts of the banking sector. If there has been irresponsibility, it has been much more systematic, sanctioned from the top, and with one clear aim in mind: the continuation and protection of economic growth' (Jackson, T., 2009: 31).

Describing this as the 'age of irresponsibility', he sets out the centrality of the international banking system in creating the problems discussed in his book. If the old vision of prosperity as continually expanding economic growth no longer works, what might an alternative vision look like? Jackson notes that since the time of Aristotle it has been recognized that more than material well-being is needed for human beings to flourish. While material resources are essential to sustain oneself, there are also vital social and psychological dimensions – relating to giving and receiving love, enjoying the respect of peers, contributing useful work, having a sense of belonging and trust in one's community – that are equally vital.

The task, Jackson argues, is about doing more with less – and it is this possibility that many people fear. For a significant proportion of the world's population, basic material well-being is a distant reality; but for many others, the notion of well-being has become an overblown addiction to 'stuff'. The pioneering work of Naomi Klein (2010) in *No Logo*, for example, reports on, and has influenced, many acts of resistance to the branded world we live in.

Reba Kennedy's blog (2012), a celebration of 'everyday simplicity', unpacks a range of terms used to describe the choice of moving to a simpler lifestyle, such as *downsizing* – a change of physical environment to increase free time, less responsibility for material things and preparation for retirement; *anti-consumerism* – taking a moral, political and activist stance against materialistic societal norms; the *Slow Movement* – maximizing appreciation of life, which started as a reaction against McDonald's restaurants in Italy and has several genres, including the Slow Food Movement and Slow Travel; *voluntary simplicity* – which involves reviewing everything for its contribution to enjoyment of life and fulfilment of purpose; and *going green* – minimizing one's ecological footprint in every way possible.

Once regarded as somewhat alternative, these life stances can also be seen as pioneering experiments carried out by innovators over the last half century (Elgin, 2010). With such a wealth of experience to draw on, these ways of being provide a vital resource for the necessary transition towards a more sustainable post-carbon future.

Interestingly, research by Fred Pearce (2012) suggests that Britons are consuming less than they did a decade ago and that similar trends can be seen across Europe. There is a reduction in water use, as well as of metals and paper, and meat-eating is falling, as is calorie consumption:

> The talk is of 'peak stuff': that beyond a certain level of economic development, people simply stop consuming so much. Technology and the course of economic evolution allow prosperity to keep rising without a linked increase in our use of energy and materials. Our demands on planetary resources stabilise – and ultimately begin to fall. Others are unconvinced, seeing in peak stuff a dangerous myth and a thinly veiled excuse to abandon efforts to limit our planetary impact. Without large-scale interventions to curb our excesses now, they argue, peak stuff, if it exists, will be too little, too late.
>
> (Pearce, 2012)

The decline in Britain's use of resources began well before the banking crisis of 2008, so it cannot be attributed to the recession. At the time of writing, the level of resource use has dropped to that of 1989. One possibility, apparent in the decline in car use among the young in the USA, is that online shopping and social media are replacing their reliance on cars. Pearce thinks it could partly be about an ageing society, where older people replace their household goods less often and don't have to commute. Whatever the reasons, it does not mean that the limits to growth have been miraculously resolved, although it might mean that at some level recognition of this has begun.

The role of education

Where in current education for sustainability might the limits to growth be looked at? I think the question highlights essential differences between what are sometimes called 'light-green' and 'dark-green' responses to the issues and to their teaching. A light-green response to social and environmental issues just scrapes the *surface*. It implies that if we were all a bit greener things would be all right – if we recycle a bit more, switch off the lights, pick up litter, perhaps do a project on polar bears. According to a light-green perspective, our lives do not need to change too much and the world just needs a bit of green tweaking and all will be well.

A dark-green response to social and environmental issues digs *deeper*. It asks more profound questions about Western economic, historical and cultural trends. It notes that changing individuals' behaviour, while important, is not enough. It argues that our social and economic systems and our rich-world lifestyles run so deep that we often fail to get to the roots of our environmental problems. It is not surface change that is needed but fundamental system change in relation to how we view growth, to how we think about nature, and to whether we care for future generations. As Huckle (2012) points out, this requires a critiquing of neo-liberalism, the current dominant ideology in the industrialized world.

I think there is a potential difficulty here in that light-green environmental thinking can seem more appropriate at primary level. I once had a cohort of students who were required to each make a presentation on an environmental issue they would like to teach about in school. I had imagined that in this diverse group their choices of topic would be diverse too, but I had never listened to so many bland presentations on water, recycling and furry animals. I felt I was witnessing the lowest common denominator in environmental education – water is important to us, recycling is a good thing and we should take care of animals – although it is true that young pupils need to learn about 'caring for the environment' and the importance of 'waste and recycling'.

What those students needed was a much more critical and creative approach to teaching and learning about the environment. How much water do we use, what do we use it for and how does this vary across the globe? Where does our water supply come from and how does water get wasted? Why is it the most precious of resources? Why do schools so often only focus on reusing and recycling? Why do they seldom explore the other R's of 'rethink, refuse and reduce', which come first? It is questions such as these that open up the topic and unfold further levels of insight and connectivity – the start, perhaps, of joined-up thinking.

Ideas for teaching
1. Ecological footprint: Four dimensions of global learning
A simple but useful model, which I have used for learning about global (or local) issues, is based on the following four dimensions of learning: Knowing, Feeling, Choosing and Acting; or, in academic language, the cognitive domain, the affective domain, decision making and a sense of agency. The four basic questions for pupils and students are: What do I need to know? What do I feel about this? What choices do I want to make? What can I do myself and with others?

In this context the four categories can be further broken down as:

1. KNOWING
   - What do we think we know/need to know about our ecological footprint?
   - What are the main causes of our ecological footprint?
   - What are some of the consequences of our footprint?
2. FEELING
   - What do I/we feel about our ecological footprint?
   - What are the concerns we may wish to share?
   - What are the hopes that we might have?
3. CHOOSING
   - What are the energy options that appear to be facing us?
   - What changes do I/we want to see in relation to our footprint?
   - What might the school do in relation to its ecological footprint?
4. ACTING
   - What do I/we therefore need to do?
   - What are others doing: school/home/community/elsewhere?
   - Who can support us in what we want to do?

2. Ecological footprint: Some key elements

Below is a summary of some key elements relating to ecological footprints. Teachers can use it as a template for planning and selecting material to suit different age groups.

RESOURCES WE USE
- The natural environment as the source of all life
- The ways in which we depend on the natural environment, for example: air to breathe, water to drink, food to eat
- Building materials, plants, animals and minerals

THE WASTE WE PRODUCE
- The natural environment as a sink for all our wastes
- The things that we dump on or in the natural environment, for example: polluted water, sewage and all sorts of rubbish
- Polluted air, waste products and greenhouse gases

A QUESTION OF BALANCE
- Not taking too much or wasting too much is 'sustainable'
- What happens if our resource use damages the environment?
- What happens if our waste disposal damages the environment?
- Taking too much and wasting too much is 'unsustainable'

A QUESTION OF FAIRNESS
- Do we take too much from environments other than our own?
- Do we dump too much waste in environments other than our own?
- Do we consume more than our fair share of the Earth's resources?
- Do we waste more than our fair share of the Earth's resources?

3. Activity: Ecological footprints

An excellent way of making the unsustainable nature of our lifestyles more visible is through mapping our own and the school's ecological footprint. The size of such a footprint can be calculated in various ways. One definition for teachers highlights three key elements and explores them in an activity: *see* Box 3.2

Box 3.2 – Treading lightly on the planet

Footprint definition

Resources we use

1. The area of land and water required to *supply all the resources* that an individual 'consumes'. By resources we mean food, housing, transport, consumer goods, water, energy and land to build on.

Waste we produce

2. The area of land and water required to *absorb the tangible wastes* produced by the individual.

3. The area of land and water required to *absorb the carbon dioxide emissions* produced when fossil fuels are burnt for energy for the individual.

This measure of consumption can also be applied to a household, school, local authority or country. Humanity's total ecological footprint is estimated at 1.5 planet Earths. The UK average footprint is 5.45 global hectares per capita and the footprint of high-income countries is five times that of lower income countries. This illuminating activity can be used with children or students to begin the process of discovery.

You will need

- A space (inside/outside) large enough for everyone to sit in a circle
- A flipchart, sugar paper/card, scissors, pens

What to do

Circle up somewhere comfortable and ask the learners to imagine that one day they come out of school to find a glass dome has come down on top of their school covering an area of 10 ha (1 ha = 100m x 100m) around it. The dome extends down into the soil, so that only light and heat can enter or escape. No air, water, food or other resource can get in; and no sewage, rubbish or other waste can get out. How long do they think they would survive? Why?

Build on their responses to reinforce that we take for granted that our local environment can interact with the rest of the world, e.g. we can transport our rubbish somewhere else to dump it, we can bring in food and building materials, our air and water will be replenished by the clouds and rain and the wind. Most of us are completely reliant on faraway sources for even our most basic needs.

Give everyone a piece of card/sugar paper and a pen. Ask them to draw carefully round their feet. Cut out the footprint outlines. Ask for examples of how their lifestyles depend on the natural environment – living processes, resources to make energy, disposal of waste, use of land, water and other natural resources to make other things and for enjoyment.

Ask learners to take one of their outlines and record, using summary words, all the things we get from the natural world to support our lifestyles – plants, animals, water, clean air, rocks and minerals, waste disposal, inspiration, peace and quiet. Now ask for examples of how their lifestyles impact on the natural environment. On the other outline, they should record all the other ways their lifestyles impact on the natural world. Explain in essence that what we get/what impact we have is how we try to measure the size of our Ecological Footprint: it's a tool to help us to measure and understand the connection between how much of nature we use and how much nature there is. If we understand the connections, we can then reduce our use and impacts. Make a display of the 'footprints'.

BIGFOOT OR LIGHTFOOT

Ask whether they think the size of people's Ecological Footprint will be the same all over the world. Why do they think that? How do they think the size might differ? Have some small and large footprint outlines, enough for each one, cut out ready (on a different colour paper). Ask them to suggest countries which may have small Ecological Footprints, and which may have large size footprints and why. Can they think why there might be a problem with this? What about outsize footprints, and how might those with the smallest footprints feel? Record inside their outlines those countries they think are relevant to the size of footprint they have been given. Check their guesses against actual footprints. Make a display.

Source: Local Footprints Project (2010)

One of the best known annual sources of information on ecological footprints is the World Wide Fund for Nature's *Living Planet Report 2013* (WWF, 2013), which contains a range of useful information that can be adapted for classroom use. Whether we choose to live within the planet's ecological limits or not, many features of life will still be changed in the future.

4. *The story of stuff*

An excellent resource for teachers and older students is 'The Story of Stuff' (2013), a 20-minute video that looks in cartoon form at the underside of our production and consumption patterns. In particular it examines the standard linear notion of extraction, production, distribution, consumption and disposal, and the impacts of each of these phases on people and environment. It brings to the fore the many processes going on in the background, which provide the 'stuff' we use in everyday life. Foregrounding these processes shows more clearly the consequences of a consumerist lifestyle. The video and other information available at www.storyofstuff.org/about/ provide a good starting point for planning work in the classroom on limits to growth.

Five things a school can do

- Staff need to become more knowledgeable about ecological footprints via www.educationscotland.gov.uk/Images/Teacher_Handbook_web_tcm4-671306.pdf.
- Time needs to be set aside for staff to share their own feelings about these matters and to discuss the implications for school policy and practice.
- Every school should have a policy on resource consumption that is monitored and has a named person to supervise its implementation.
- Awareness of these matters should be introduced into curriculum and practice in such a way that they become the norm for both children and teachers.
- Questioning rich-world assumptions is vital and best approached through geographical comparisons with living conditions in less economically developed countries.

Part Two

Facing the challenge

2

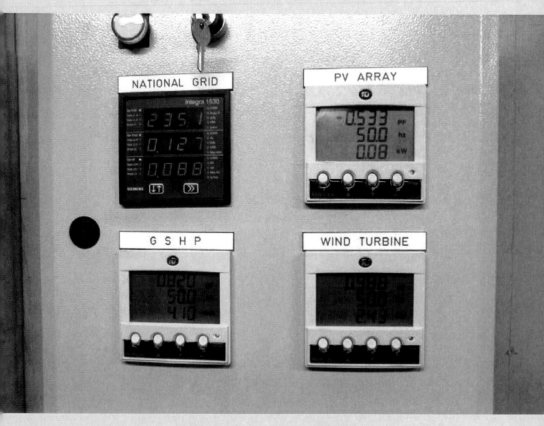

Data panel at Cockermouth School

Chapter 4
Acknowledging feelings

Anxiety and denial

Human beings respond to difficult situations in all sorts of ways. For example, denial is a common response to situations that make us feel uncomfortable. It is one of the ways in which we deal – or avoid dealing – with aspects of life we don't like, whether in ourselves, our family, a relationship or the world at large. We often prefer not to know about things that we think will be painful; but the dilemma is that this avoidance of them creates blind spots and zones of self-deception. The psychology of denial also occurs at institutional, national and international levels – perhaps in relation to terrorist attacks, or reports of hunger and malnutrition, or the dangers of climate change. Such psychic numbing denies the seriousness of problems – 'It's not really that bad'; 'I'm sure that scientists will find a way to sort it out'; 'There's nothing I can do about it anyway.'

Denial therefore saves us from having to face up to a problem, take responsibility or think about the consequences of our actions (or inactions). Sandra Postel recognizes that:

> Psychology as much as science will ... determine the planet's fate, because action depends on overcoming denial, among the most paralysing of human responses. While it affects most of us to varying degrees, denial often runs particularly deep among those with heavy stakes in the status quo ... This kind of denial can be as dangerous to society and the natural environment as an alcoholic's denial is to his or her own health and family ... rather than face the truth, denial's victims choose slow suicide.
>
> (Postel, 1992: 4)

Denial is an understandable response to the sheer *enormity* of some of the issues in the world. I remember a colleague saying to me once: 'I've got an ill child at home, a father with dementia, a car that won't start and you want me to worry about the world!' But there's a difference between denial of wider issues and needing to put them on the shelf for later consideration.

One of the dilemmas we collectively face is that the future increasingly feels like a troubled place, but we have no choice other than to go there.

Thinking about this, and about the local–global issues that confront us, can be worrying, frightening, puzzling, annoying, challenging, exciting and even downright dangerous. We are, whether we choose to be aware of it or not, confronted by a range of emotions that we may actually not wish to know about, let alone feel.

Grappling with the emotional is often harder than rational analysis, as David Orr observed.

> For all of our information and communications prowess, we talk too little about our motives and feelings in relation to our occupations and professions. I recall, for example, a conversation in which a group of distinguished ecologists and environmentalists were asked to describe the sources of their beliefs. In trying to describe their deepest emotions as if they were the result of carefully considered career plans, these otherwise eloquent people descended into a pit of muddled incoherence. But as the conversation continued, deeply moving stories about experiences of the most personal kind began to emerge.
>
> (Orr, 1994: 45)

The priorities of the Scientific Revolution and the Enlightenment valorized the intellect and made it the arbiter of all things. What is sometimes known as the affective domain, i.e. that which concerns feelings and emotions, thus became seen as the territory of women or of the Romantic poets and philosophers. The query I heard once as to whether or not a workshop would be 'touchy feely' highlights a 200-year distinction between head and heart, intellect and emotions. Yet unless we feel deeply we cannot truly live. We cannot be truly present to life, to our partners, to our children, to our students or to our world. In order to tackle issues such as climate change, we need to *care*. Yet when I suggested to a colleague that learning about global issues involved the affective domain as much as the intellect he replied: 'I don't expect to have to be a therapist in my work.' But useful insights can be gained from the field of therapy if we want to understand our emotional responses to situations, our hopes and fears for the future and how we deal with them.

Did you grow up in a family where you were encouraged to express your emotions, both positive and negative emotions, or did you learn, as I did by default, that emotions are not something we talk about? If you have learnt that emotions are to be suppressed, you cannot be present to the emotional life of your students and are thus only half present to them. Freud and others have observed that the experiences we have as babies and in childhood stay with us throughout our lives. Did you learn that other people are to be trusted or to be feared? Did you learn that the world is a fearful place or a place where you can feel secure? Did your childhood experiences encourage optimism or pessimism in relation to the human experience?

John Heron (1999) argues that our initial years always leave us with 'archaic and existential' anxiety. Thus our experience of birth, of parenting, of our siblings, lays down deep subconscious responses to life – as to whether we expect encounters with other people to be safe or unsafe, or whether we expect love to be conditional or unconditional. Heron suggests, however, that there are two more categories of anxiety aroused by threatening issues that are more wide ranging. One is *cultural and planetary anxiety*:

> The sorts of concerns which give rise to this are: Is the society in which I live making the most of its human and physical resources? Is it a just society? ... What can I do about human rights abuses in so many parts of the world? ... Can we cross the division between rich and poor nations? Are we taking care of our planet?
>
> (Heron, 1999: 67)

The other is *transcendental anxiety*:

> The sorts of concerns which give rise to this are: Is there a God? What is my relationship with such a reality? What is my destiny? How have I come into being? ... What is the ground of my identity? Who am I? What happens to me after death?

Heron goes on to point out that the issues giving rise to our archaic and existential anxiety are subordinate to the wider concerns, which give rise to cultural/planetary and transcendental anxiety. He concludes:

> Looked at as positive stimuli, cultural/planetary anxiety and transcendental anxiety offer two very fundamental and complementary challenges. The challenge of shaping a new kind of society, both locally and globally, which cares for the planetary environment and manifests social justice. The challenge of living awarely within the conscious experiential field of a multi-dimensional universe. Both these challenges provide an exhilarating context for the further development and application of experiential learning.
>
> (Heron, 1999: 68)

In his work Heron demonstrates the depth of the affective domain, whether it is acknowledged or not, and the way in which our deepest anxieties embrace both the personal and the planetary. But what happens when some of the issues we are confronted with produce levels of anxiety that we cannot bear? In our personal lives this is where denial often comes in. In situations of domestic abuse, for example, the denial might take the form of justifying thoughts such as: 'He's not an alcoholic, he just likes a drink'; 'He's a good man, he doesn't hit me very hard'. Stanley Cohen, in *States of Denial*, explores the human responses to knowing about atrocities and suffering:

> Denial is understood as an unconscious defence mechanism for coping with guilt, anxiety and other disturbing emotions aroused by reality. The psyche blocks off information that is literally unthinkable or unbearable. The unconscious sets up a barrier which prevents the thought from reaching conscious knowledge. Information and memories slip into an inaccessible region of the mind.
>
> (Cohen, 2001: 5)

Robert Jay Lifton and Greg Mitchell (1995) studied the way in which the precedent of the atomic bombing of Hiroshima in 1945 was processed individually and collectively over the next fifty years in the USA. The scale of the destruction and the fear of nuclear war as a result of the Cold War superpower arms race led to 'psychic numbing' on a national (and global) scale in the face of possible apocalypse. The notion that human life might be extinguished, the authors comment, led to a sense of doom and futurelessness. Their interviews suggest a merging of nuclear fear with other apocalyptic threats, such as environmental destruction and global warming.

Kari Norgaard (2011) found in her research with a rural Norwegian community that people avoided thinking about climate change in part because it led to feelings of helplessness and guilt and to fears of profound vulnerability. The emotional management techniques people used to avoid discussion of climate change were particularly pronounced among educators, among men and among public figures. Individual denial, she points out, is socially constructed so that it becomes 'impossible' for people to engage in any discussion or social activism in relation to global warming because this broaches social and cultural norms.

Shierry Nicholsen, in *The Love of Nature and the End of the World*, argues that:

> The current situation calls for what Wilfred Bion calls *binocular vision*: we must pay attention both to the possibility of catastrophe and to the alternatives. If we do not face the genuine possibility of further catastrophe, we cannot envision a response. That is why

Lifton and Mitchell caution us to imagine the end of the world. One reason we do not let ourselves imagine such a possibility, however, is that we have ... 'no pre-existing place in the mind for it'.

(Nicholsen, 2002:155)

One of the concepts that equips us to face adversity, she argues, is the continuity of life through time. That there might be no future for our children and grandchildren to inhabit fills us with anxiety. But it is this very concern for those who come after that impels us to find a realistic hope for the future.

It is only when we can reflect critically and creatively on the future that we can help pupils, students and colleagues fully to understand the importance of global citizenship and sustainability education. It is only when we acknowledge the anxiety that issues such as climate change engender within us that we can begin to move forward. Only then can we be truly present to optimism and hope. As long as we avoid thinking about the future and the feelings it may generate, we contribute to a culture of denial. It is a basic tenet of psychotherapy that we repress material that we do not want to be consciously aware of, whether the traumas of childhood or the difficulties of adult life. As part of a therapeutic process the patient has to re-engage with these 'split-off 'experiences and integrate them healthily into everyday life so that old wounds are gradually healed (Heron, 1999). From that healing can come a sense of empowerment and an ability to face new situations with a sense of agency.

Owning the affective domain

The affective domain – the world of feelings and emotions, attitudes and values – is as important to life and learning as the cognitive domain of thought and intellect. This chapter has argued that although avoidance and denial, from the personal to the planetary, can protect us from anxiety and discomfort they also make it more difficult for us to deal with such situations. Being more open to and aware of emotions makes one much more open to life, more aware of the pain but also of the joy of being human. Humanistic psychology takes a holistic view of the person, that to be most fully alive we need to be aware of head (cognitive), heart (feelings), body (physical) and spirit (intuition). It is having access to our feelings that puts us in touch with the drive for positive change. That desire to change things can be about one's own personal growth and about the world. John Rowan writes: 'Personal growth is what happens when a healthy person with no very obvious problems decides on a process of self-exploration for self-understanding, simply in order to be more able' (1998: 19). It is about taking responsibility for ourselves. Only when we begin to do so can we become fully human:

> What we are trying to do all the time is to bring something which is hidden out into the open a bit more, so that we have a chance to see just how big or small it is, how important or unimportant, how shallow or deep, how much feeling is attached to it or bound up with it.
>
> (Rowan, 1998: 102)

One of the most useful representations of the painful layers of human emotional life is Rowan's 'affect tree' (1998: 103). At the top of the tree (the twigs) are uncomfortable feelings such as sadness, criticality, hurt and nervousness, which we experience in everyday situations and in relation to global issues. We can recognize these emotional states in ourselves and others. One reason why we find them uncomfortable is because underlying them are even more powerful feelings of grief, anger, pain, anxiety and fear (the branches). Understandably, we often don't want to visit these emotions, and socialization has also often taught us that to express them in public is inappropriate. So we are ashamed of such feelings and repress them. It is often seen as particularly 'uncool' to express anxiety, pain or grief about the state of the world.

The role of education

How then to be more open to our emotional lives, so we release the mental and emotional energy we use to repress unwanted emotions? The organization Antidote defines emotional literacy as 'the practice of thinking individually and collectively about how emotions shape our actions, and of using emotional understanding to enrich our thinking' (2003: v). Emotional understanding or misunderstanding affects every aspect of daily life, whether in relation to oneself or the wider world:

> Being encouraged to communicate positively with others can help us work towards states of calm well-being where we start to understand what we are feeling. We can take in feedback from others, allowing their smiles, grimaces, gestures and words to help us know ourselves, to distinguish our different emotional states, to reflect on how these states emerge from our experiences of situations. Out of these multiple experiences of human interaction, we develop the capacity to access, understand and respond appropriately to a wide range of emotional states in ourselves

and others. We become able to think both about what we are experiencing emotionally and about anything else that comes up. This generates the possibility of our thinking and feeling capacities working together.

(Antidote, 2003: 13)

It is this link between thinking and feeling that provides the underpinning for social and emotional learning in schools. If, as pupil, student or teacher, we have no way of processing feelings such as insecurity and anxiety, we feel powerless and unprotected and disconnect our thinking from our feelings. Obviously this does not help in any social or learning situation we are in (Rose *et al.*, 2013). Antidote sees emotional literacy as the bridge between the cognitive zone and the affective zone:

When the bridge is well maintained, there is free traffic between these two areas of the brain. The information received in the emotional zone can be taken in, thought about, reflected upon, used to shape our responses and enrich our ideas. There is a possibility of interaction that is alive, fruitful and buzzing. Picture the situation, by contrast, when the bridge has been neglected ... It might be possible for some communication to take place, but it involves hopping tentatively across jagged fragments of the old bridge – the process is slow, dangerous and inconsistent. People lack the capacity to use the rich resources of intuition that their emotions provide or to think before they act ... The more stress individuals have experienced or are experiencing in their current situation, the more likely they are to find themselves trapped on one side or other of the river, without the capacity to get across.

(Antidote, 2003: 14)

The affective domain relates to human interaction but, as this chapter has indicated, equally to our concerns and anxieties about society generally and the big issues dealt with in this book. It is difficult for both adults and young people to share their fears and anxieties about such issues if they are discouraged from doing so in relation to personal and interpersonal issues. Such discouragement can be overt, but it is more often unspoken. It is therefore important to look at some of the key skills of emotional literacy as they relate to the personal and interpersonal.

It is far easier for young people to be open to feeling concern about global issues such as climate change and peak oil when they are emotionally literate – and education has a crucial role in enhancing pupils' and students' self-esteem and emotional literacy, and thus in enhancing their ability to be *present* to the world. Teachers need certain key qualities in order to model effective social and emotional learning, whether for children, students or colleagues.

Humanistic psychologist Carl Rogers argues that to get the best out of learners, every teacher's repertoire must include three vital skills (Rogers and Freiberg, 1994). The first is *acceptance*, that is, the ability to be non-judgemental and accept the pupil for who they are. This is based on making the vital distinction between a pupil and their behaviour, since blaming a child makes them feel attacked and rejected, which is certainly not conducive to learning. There is an important difference between saying, 'I'm tired of you always making a mess' and 'I don't like this mess on the floor'. The former is blaming the pupil; the latter draws attention to the result of the behaviour without attaching blame to it. The second skill is *genuineness*, which requires an honest appraisal of oneself as a teacher and how one comes across in the classroom. For example, are you present to pupils as yourself or do you hide behind a mask of authority? The third skill is *empathy*, the ability to put oneself in someone else's shoes to acquire a real sense of what they may be feeling. When students feel accepted for who they are, see the real you and know you try to understand their feelings, more meaningful interactions and deeper learning become possible.

When my students were dubious about the value of such skills, I asked them to reflect on their own schooling and to identify examples of these skills being present or absent in their interaction with teachers. What they reported was that the warmth engendered by the presence of these skills had greatly enhanced their learning and left positive feelings, which they wanted to share. At the same time the absence or opposite of such skills had led to thwarted learning and painfully diminished self-esteem. Children don't miss a trick. Having been away for a day, a primary teacher I knew asked his class how they had got on with their stand-in teacher. 'Oh, he shouted at us!' they said. 'But I shout at you too,' said their class teacher, to which came the reply, 'Yes, but we know you don't mean it!'

Another route into discussing emotional literacy with students is to look at how it feels when they have to work on a task in small groups. Most students are nervous at first when asked to work in groups – nervous about whom they might be with, whether they will be listened to, or whether they will have anything to say. But in these present difficult times and the times to come, being able to get on well with others may rank as not just a life skill but also a survival skill. To be able to access the affective domain for ourselves and with others makes it possible to explore the feelings that arise in relation to big issues, such as climate change and peak oil.

To be human is to interact with other people, to relate to others, often in groups. People will have different reasons for being in a group, will want different things out of it, may not get on equally well with others in that group. While we may not think about it consciously, we need a range of social and emotional skills to relate well with others, to come to agreements, to achieve common goals. This is particularly the case when we have to cooperate with others to achieve a specific goal, as in a discussion group or when involved in environmental or social action. The three 'checklists' near the end of this chapter provide guidelines that teachers can use with pupils or tutors with their students. These interpersonal skills are vital to facilitate supportive relationships with others, especially when dealing with difficult issues such as climate change.

'Circle time', when done well, provides another excellent opportunity for learning some of the skills of emotional literacy (Circle Time, 2013). I used it with one of my student groups to open each weekly session, knowing that this process is also as valuable for adults as young people. We had previously discussed the effect the layout of the room can have on class interaction and learning, so they were disconcerted when they came in and found the chairs set out in a single circle. Once everyone had arrived I asked what the worried faces were about, and the response was that they felt exposed to everyone else's gaze and had nowhere to hide. We then looked at the non-hierarchical nature of a circle and the value of visibility of the community of learners. Since the students were already familiar with the ground rules for working in small groups, I suggested only one person should speak at a time and that everyone listen attentively but without commenting on what others shared. We used a stone from the beach that fitted into the palm of the hand as the 'token' that allowed someone to speak.

Thus the circle time session began for these students, most of whom were going to be primary teachers. 'What does this new experience feel like?' I asked. Their responses ranged from paralysis and discomfort to curiosity and relief. After everyone had spoken, the stone was laid in the centre of the circle and whoever wanted to comment on the process we had been through was free to pick it up. Over the weeks, starting in the circle became accepted as the norm, a place where experiences and feelings could be expressed freely without criticism. Students began to look forward to the experience and expressed disappointment on the one occasion when it couldn't be done. We talked about how circle time could be used in the classroom and about examples of what they had experienced on school practice. Some teachers had used the process to comment on what children had shared, not always helpfully, and some had failed to clarify the ground rules. For her dissertation, one student examined how two different teachers used circle time in the school where she had been teaching. When we met to discuss her study, she said she felt it might not work as only one teacher demonstrated good practice. I pointed out that as she was a budding authority on circle time, it was equally valuable to analyse poor practice.

Such examples of cooperative working with others illustrate ways in which issues of voice, self-esteem and emotional learning can be approached and eventually welcomed into participants' lives. As my students soon saw, many of their fears about engaging with the emotional domain arose from experiences during their own schooling. What they now wanted to see and fully contribute to was the life of an emotionally literate school (Park and Tew, 2007). Such schools are essential to positive learning experiences, where the climate of discussion can more fully support children's concerns for the future.

These interpersonal skills are absolutely vital to effective classroom interaction, both between teacher and pupil and among pupils. Developing such skills creates greater acceptance of and empathy towards others, and increased self-esteem, emotional literacy and social cohesion. Head and heart are to be equally valued; both are at the centre of critical and creative learning. Teachers, pupils and students need such interpersonal skills so they can discuss issues such as those highlighted in this book constructively and sensitively and develop a keen sense of agency.

Ideas for teaching

Feeling safe in new situations, being able to speak and listen thoughtfully, reaching agreement when working with others – all are vital to the smooth running of a classroom, school or community. These skills are vital to the effective functioning of all human relationships, but are seldom emphasized in educational contexts. They greatly facilitate coming to agreement (or begging to differ) about issues such as climate change, peak oil or the limits to growth. The prompts below highlight some of the interpersonal skills that underpin effective learning, because of how they pay equal attention to the cognitive and the affective domains.

1. Working with others
HOW DOES IT FEEL?

All sorts of things come up for learners in a new group or situation. Some of the feelings may be: 'Will I like these people?' 'Will they like me?' 'What if someone criticizes me?' Or, 'I'm looking forward to this.' 'I might learn something new.' 'I might make new friends.' Often it's a mix of the two.

Either way, strong feelings can come up. This is normal. The important thing is to pay attention to such feelings, to listen to them to see what they are saying. The affective domain is just as important as the cognitive domain in education – and life.

Some of the feelings that come up in a new situation will be to do with a sense of safety. Does it feel OK to be here? Are these people I want to be with? If one has been able to choose who one is with, this choice is often based on who one feels best supported and respected by.

Ground rules

It is difficult to work well with others if one is feeling insecure, so setting up ground rules that give the group a sense of security is essential. Ground rules can be drawn up by the teacher, tutor or group members. Here are five essential ones.

- *Speaking* – only one person speaks at a time; this could be as a result of putting a hand up or agreeing to take it in turns to speak.
- *Listening* – it is important to listen attentively to what the other person is saying and not interrupt them.
- *Not judging* – listen without making judgements about the other person, respecting their rights to their views, opinions and feelings.
- *Sharing* – no one person should dominate the discussion, no one should be left out, and everyone should be encouraged to contribute.
- *Voice* – it's not about saying the right thing or having an answer; rather, it's about 'finding one's voice', which may just be to share what one is feeling with the group.

A shared task

The most important thing in a task-orientated group is to reach agreement on what the goal is and how best to achieve it. But there will always be a tension between individual and group needs and one may have to put some of one's own needs aside.

This does not mean ignoring people's needs. They could take it in turns at the beginning to say briefly how they feel about the task: 'Is there anything I need to say *before* I can be really present to the task?'

2. Speaking and listening

Sharing feelings

It often helps participants to check periodically on how they feel about the task. Responses might include: 'I feel really excited about working together on this'; 'I feel worried about the task we have to do'; or 'I feel nervous about having anything to say about climate change'.

Such statements do not necessarily require an answer, but they do let others know what is being felt and take it into account. Feelings are out in the open – feelings that might hinder achievement of the task if not expressed. They also often strike a chord of sympathy with others in the group.

SHARING OPINIONS

For a group to achieve its task everyone needs to contribute, so everybody needs to share their thoughts, feelings and opinions. Some participants might feel they do not have anything to say, or they might be nervous about sharing ideas and feelings with others.

Whatever the topic is everyone will have *some* response to it, so participants should spend a moment or two jotting down any questions, ideas or experiences that feel relevant. It's OK to be tentative about what one's first comments are. Often it's only in the actual process of discussion that ideas become clear.

It's best to present one's views lightly, as one may want to refine or alter them later. Similarly, other people's starting points may not be where they finish up.

ACTIVE LISTENING

Sometimes it's important to remind participants about the ground rules, as they make the group feel in a safe place in which to experiment and try out ideas.

Active listening means listening carefully to what someone is saying whether one agrees with it or not. It means not interrupting or spending the time thinking about a reply. If one is uncertain, check with the speaker that one has understood what they are saying correctly.

This can be done by summarizing briefly what one feels the speaker has said: 'What I heard you say was … .' (This is important because what we *think* we have heard is not always what the speaker intended.) The speaker then knows they've been attended to carefully and can clarify points if needed. When people feel listened to and respected the task becomes easier and more fun.

3. Coming to agreement

WORKING COOPERATIVELY

If a group follows all the strategies described above – and this takes practice – one is well on the way to good cooperative working. This involves considering different ways to set about a task and agreeing on the best one. If people feel safe in a group they are less likely to mind making compromises.

Working cooperatively doesn't mean that everyone has to agree. One can work cooperatively and supportively to identify the main differences of opinion and to clarify arguments for and against different opinions. Cooperative working helps to bring out the best in others. Developing these interpersonal skills takes time, but in learning to work cooperatively, synergy can build so that the insight and output of the group feels more than the sum of its parts.

Never underestimate the value of these interpersonal skills because through them pupils learn both to find their own voice and also to practise respect for others. They are essential – to effective learning, to working with others, for being present to both head and heart, and for discussing the big issues we are now facing and how we feel about them. Whether as teachers or learners, or both, we cannot fully acknowledge the feelings created by issues such as global warming unless we acknowledge ourselves and others as emotional beings.

Five things a school can do

- Staff need to become knowledgeable about emotional literacy via a brief presentation or text such as Park and Tew's *Emotional Literacy Pocketbook*.
- Time needs to be set aside for staff to share their own feelings about these matter and to discuss the implications for school policy and practice.
- Every school should have a policy on emotional literacy. This needs to be monitored and have a named person to supervise its implementation.
- Emotional literacy should be introduced into curriculum and practice in such a way that they become the norm for both children and teachers.
- Both pupils and teachers should be consulted on the policy and the value and effectiveness of it for the school.

Chapter 5

Questioning the future

Tomorrow has been cancelled

When I ran a national curriculum project in the UK on teaching about global issues I generally started the session with the following activity.

Pairs of participants were given a set of cards, each bearing a statement beginning 'Schools should help young people explore contemporary issues relating to ...'. The issues I chose then were: the environment, wealth and poverty, peace and conflict, race and racism, gender and sexism, children's voices, political debates, globalization, the future. The pairs were asked to rank the cards, after coming to some agreement about which issues they felt were most important (and which least) for schools to teach. The ensuing discussions were reported back to the whole group. It made a lively start to the day. After using the activity with a good many groups I realized that the same issue always came last – the future.

One of my questions consequently became: 'But why did you rank the future last?' The teachers' answers ranged from 'because it hasn't happened yet' and 'I don't know anything about it' to 'it's not part of the curriculum' and 'I don't think my Head would like it.' Yet it seemed to me that all teaching was about preparing young people for their futures, so this became a subsequent focus for my work. Long before climate change and peak oil had been identified, educators were concerned about global issues and trends and how to help young people understand their impact on daily life (*see* the Introduction). But trends, if they become more pronounced, will always have future impacts – yet the future seemed to be a no go area in education, another example of denial.

This chapter therefore begins by acknowledging this missing dimension in much of education, while also considering what it looks like when it is present. How do people think about the future?

What I found was that while some people thought deeply about possible futures, because it was an important element in their work – town planners, business analysts and environmental activists, for example – for the vast majority of people life seemed too busy to think far beyond the present. Clearly, the future is very much part of our everyday lives, whenever we consult our diaries, take out a mortgage, choose a birthday present or wonder about our pensions. These activities reflect personal futures as against wider societal futures. If I ever mentioned I had a particular interest in the future people would generally say: 'Oh, you mean astrology' or 'Betting on the horses are you?'

One of the biggest cross-cultural surveys on people's views of the future reported that the tendency to think about it was not very developed among respondents (Ornauer *et al.*, 1976). People tended to focus on developments in science and technology, and pessimistic visions of the future were better developed than optimistic ones. The conclusion noted that:

> For the nations in our sample the future seemed to be somehow synonymous with a technological future. The future is seen in technical terms, not in terms of culture, human enrichment, social equality, social justice, or in terms of international affairs ... People may also think in terms of social future but regard it as unchangeable. But it seems more probable that they have only been trained to think technologically and have no other type of thoughts as a response to the stimulus 'future'; or at least have not been trained to express any other thoughts. And this will then become self-reinforcing since no one will be stimulated by others to think about social futures.
>
> (Galtung, 1976: 56–7)

I wonder how similar or different the findings would be if such a survey were done today? Johan Galtung's notion, that people didn't think about the wider future because they hadn't been taught how to, might appear to cut across the notion of denial. However, the survey was carried out in a decade when the Cold War threatened nuclear annihilation. Perhaps this partly explains why pessimistic visions of the future were better developed than optimistic ones.

Noel Gough (1990: 298–310) examined a range of educational documents in order to see what images of the future they contained. He found that 'Even a cursory analysis of educational discourse reveals its temporal asymmetry. That is, by comparison to the future, the temporal categories of past and present receive more frequent and more explicit attention.' He argued, however, that all educational writers implicitly convey some notion of the future even if this is difficult to discern. These tend, he found, to fall into three categories – tacit inferences, token invocations or taken-for-granted assumptions.

'Tacit futures' are those implied but never clearly stated, for example a passing reference to preparation for adult life. Tacit futures are virtually invisible to the untrained eye, says Gough. 'Token futures' are a bit more visible but tend to be rhetorical references only, for example conferences in the 1990s entitled 'Education for the Twenty-First Century' and '2020 Vision'. 'Taken-for-granted' futures are the most visible, but they propose only one particular view of the future as if no alternatives exist. The most common view is that continued economic growth is the answer to all known human problems.

Having been involved in the international field of futures education for many years I can look back and assess what impact there may have been in the UK (Hicks, 2006a, 2012b). While it is possible to talk about the evolution of futures education internationally, practice in the UK is still at a pre-emergent stage. It remains to be seen whether teachers and teacher educators will recognize the value of futures thinking to their own work. It remains to be seen whether potentially interested parties, such as geography teachers and sustainability educators, will develop a critical futures strand within their own teaching and research at a time when creative and critical thinking about the future is urgently needed at all levels of education. Box 5.1 summarizes some of the lessons that can be learnt from the UK experience so far.

BOX 5.1 – THINKING ABOUT THE FUTURE IN UK SCHOOLS

GENERAL
- It could be said there is little educational interest in futures in the UK because there is little familiarity with the academic field of futures studies or futures more generally in society. Whilst this may be one reason for its neglect there are also other factors at play.
- Firstly, the future is something that most people tend to leave to others because the pressures of daily life feel more than enough to deal with. There seems little time to think about the future because the demands of the immediate present always edge it out.
- Secondly, the future may become of greater concern if it suddenly appears threatening or dangerous to one's family or community, but at the same time this may lead to denial as a way of avoiding feelings of responsibility.
- Thirdly, there are of course those who take a wider interest in futures but this is generally because they are either futurists or activists seeking to change society for the better. Whilst the first group is not widely known to the public the latter group are dismissed by many as merely 'protestors'.

EDUCATION
- Teachers, teacher trainers and educational publishers still find it difficult to grasp the nature of futures and futures thinking because they take it to be too abstract for the classroom and/or they are uncertain about who should take responsibility for such a dimension in the curriculum, i.e. the curriculum is still viewed largely in 'subject' terms
- What educational interest there is tends to be in the form of tacit or taken-for-granted futures since mainstream education sees the most important drivers of change as the knowledge economy and future developments in technology (*see* penultimate point below).
- However, progressive educators concerned with issues of inequality and injustice, global citizenship and education for sustainability, are more likely to ask questions about the directions in which contemporary society is heading and to propose alternatives for the future.

IDEOLOGY
- Education in society always reflects the values of the dominant political ideology, which in the West today is that of neoliberalism. This advocates an unfettered technocentric and business-as-usual future based on free market economics, constant consumerism and narcissistic individualism. This ideology is inevitably reproduced in schools and underpins western views of the future.
- However, other more radical ideologies have been influencing society from the margins in the form of global social movements. Amongst the most important are those to do with poverty, gender, human rights, globalisation, the environment and climate change. Their proponents often try to live as if they were experiments from the preferred future that they wish to create.

Source: Hicks (2012b)

Terms such as 'futures education' are useful at an international level, because they signal a common interest and a shared expertise. At national and local levels, however, such terms can become obstacles. In the UK it is more appropriate to talk about the need for students to develop a 'futures perspective', because that is closer to the language of teachers and more immediately understandable. In the face of the issues discussed in this book, and in relation to sustainability more widely, teachers urgently need to help pupils develop a more futures-orientated perspective.

Reinstating the future

The academic field of futures studies gradually emerged after World War Two. Sohail Inayatullah (1993: 236) notes that it 'largely straddles two dominant modes of knowledge – the technical concerned with predicting the future and the humanist concerned with developing a good society'. Key resources in this field include texts such as the *Knowledge Base of Futures Studies* (Slaughter, 2005), *Foundations of Futures Studies* (Bell, 2010) and *Advancing Futures* (Dator, 2002).

Wendell Bell (2010: 73) argues that the purpose of futures studies is to 'discover or invent, examine, evaluate and propose possible, probable and preferable futures'. He continues: 'futurists seek to know: what can or could be (the possible), what is likely to be (the probable), and what ought to be (the preferable)'. James Dator elaborates further:

> The future cannot be studied because the future does not exist. Futures studies does not … pretend to study the future. It studies ideas about the future… (which) often serve as the basis for actions in the present…Different groups often have very different images of the future. Men's images may differ from women's. Western images may differ from non-Western, and so on.
>
> One of the main tasks of futures studies is to identify and examine the major alternative futures which exist at any given time and place. The future cannot be predicted, but preferred futures can and should be envisioned, invented, implemented, continuously evaluated, revised, and re-envisioned. Thus, another major task of futures studies is to facilitate individuals and groups in formulating, implementing, and re-envisioning their preferred futures.
>
> (Dator, 2005)

The field of futures studies is thus a rich and vital resource for anyone interested in the possible futures that may occur as a consequence of past and present human activity. Where are we going?' and 'Where do we want to get to?' are questions as old as time. An appreciation of futures studies can provide a variety of frameworks and methodologies for thinking about and analysing futures, and it can be adapted for use in many different educational contexts.

Popular books that claim to be about the future appear periodically. They range from whimsical nonsense to free-market fantasies about technological cornucopias. They may be useful for passing the time and seeing how imaginative authors can be, but they seldom refer to futures studies or acknowledge its existence. I think this may be because, at some level, everyone thinks they can speculate about the future as well as the next person. However, writing that is grounded in the work of real 'futurists' is important. Here are two good examples.

Christopher Barnatt's exploration of things one should know about the future opens like this:

> While technology may still allow us to do many incredible things, there is also a distinct possibility that shortages of oil, fresh water and other natural resources will start to constrain our lifestyles. In a little more than a decade we may therefore descend into a spiral of industrial decline. Like it or not, we are entering an age of unparalleled technological possibility just at the moment when the cupboard of Planet Earth is starting to run bare.
>
> Perhaps more than at any other time in history, the future of advanced civilisation now hangs in the balance. Without a crystal ball it is impossible to predict precisely what lies ahead. However, by studying known challenges, next-generation technologies and current trends, we can gain some insight into a range of possible futures. We can then act to make our most favoured vision of tomorrow a reality. Or in other words, we can use future gazing as a tool for shaping the future.
>
> (Barnatt, 2012: x – xi)

The book's five themes provide a useful outline map of current futures issues: The End of the Age of Plenty (peak oil, climate change, peak water, food shortages, resource depletion); The Next Industrial Wave (3D printing, nano-technology, genetic modification, synthetic biology); Fuelling the Third Millennium (electric vehicles, wind and wave power, solar energy, nuclear fusion); Computing and Inorganic Life (cloud computing, artificial intelligence, augmented reality, quantum computing); Humanity 2.0 (genetic medicine, bioprinting, cybernetic enhancement, life extension).

In *The Rough Guide to the Future* Jon Turney covers the following ground:

- the hopes, fears and best predictions of fifty of the world's leading futurologists and scientists

- a survey of new technological horizons: nanobots, cryonics, space colonies and the Internet of Things
- a review of the most feasible disasters: oil shocks, global pandemics, religious conflicts, earthquakes and tsunamis
- the outlook for health, from robot surgery to a cure for the common cold
- past visions of the future, from Nostradamus and the Oracle at Delphi to Jules Verne and H.G. Wells.

(Turney, 2010)

Both books provide useful maps of key issues that confront us now and which will influence the lives of present and future generations. It is important to recall the distinction made by Wendell Bell between possible, probable and preferable futures. All of the futures described here are *possible*, in that they could come about in some form or another. The crucial distinction is between *probable* futures, the ones that seem most likely to emerge, and *preferable* futures, the ones we would most like to see come about. The main argument of the present book is that the hazards of climate change, peak oil and resource depletion, rather than merely being possible futures, are now probable futures in some form. And we need to be able to envision the preferable future – zero carbon and sustainable – that will enable society to survive such difficulties (*see* Chapter 9).

A great deal of work has been done on thinking about preferable futures, but it often shows no insight into the support that futures studies can offer such ventures. Futurists can provide various conceptual frameworks that help facilitate thinking about the future (some of which have already been mentioned above). However, dreaming about the possibility of a better future is an inherent element of the human condition, as are the questions 'Where have we come from?', 'Where are we now?', 'Where do we want to get to?' Some of the most important insights have come from the major social movements since the 1960s, which have challenged various aspects of the status quo. Although the Establishment has usually regarded being 'anti' something as a negative force and therefore to be shunned, such movements have begun when people identified a wrong or injustice in society that needs to be challenged. When the accepted channels for change fail to respond or attempt to belittle such concerns, then people do what they have always done, which is take to the streets.

The various social movements of the last fifty years include the civil rights movement in the United States (the right for African Americans to vote), protests against the Vietnam War, the environmental movement, the women's movement, the peace movement, the anti-racist movement, the human-rights movement, the anti-nuclear movement, the anti-globalization movement, the climate change movement and the Transition Movement (OneWorld, 2013). Such loosely structured mass movements have often involved millions of people across the planet. At different times different groups and issues are in the headlines. All are fighting for different aspects of a more just, equitable and sustainable future. The fact that issues of gender, race and human rights, for example, are seen as important today has as much to do with these social movements as the work done by others acting within civil society. Many of the things we take for granted – the right to vote, safety at work, freedom of speech – only came about because our ancestors also had visions of a better future for themselves and their children, which they were prepared to fight for. So we too must ask: What sort of future do we want for *our* children and grandchildren?

The role of education

Given the seriousness of current global issues, one would expect teachers and teacher trainers to take a particular interest in the sort of future their charges might have to live in (probable futures) or would like to live in (preferable futures), yet until recently this has not been the case. Nearly forty years ago Toffler, in his excellent book *Learning for Tomorrow* (1974), wrote:

> All education springs from images of the future and all education creates images of the future. Thus all education, whether so intended or not, is a preparation for the future. Unless we understand the future for which we are preparing, we may do tragic damage to those we teach. Unless we understand the powerful psychological role played by images of the future in motivating – or de-motivating – the learner, we cannot effectively overhaul our schools, colleges or universities, no matter what innovations we introduce.
>
> (Toffler, 1974: cover)

Excellent materials are available from the academic field of futures studies (Bell, 2010; Slaughter, 2005; Inayatullah, 2013) but they are seldom consulted in teacher education. Ideas and resources for teachers are available across the sectors, for example, Page (2000) on the early years, or Hicks and Holden (2007) and Hicks (2012a) at primary level. In the UK it is geographers, both primary and secondary, who have been the first to include a futures perspective in their work (Hicks, 2007, 2013). Given the long-standing interest in teaching about global issues in schools, it should include a fuller exploration of their probable future impact.

Debra Bateman's (2012) research in Australia on a group of primary-school teachers found their notions of the future to be stereotyped and uncritical. The teachers were uncertain about what a futures perspective was or how it might be introduced into the classroom. During supportive ongoing professional development work with the researcher (herself a trained primary teacher) they remained worried about how such a perspective might be achieved. However, on introducing the work they had prepared for their classes they found the pupils to be knowledgeable, excited and eager to plunge into issues that really mattered to them: how the future might be, how they wanted it to be, and how, with others, they could work towards the changes they sought. Perhaps children know more than adults.

One of the strongest future-orientated statements in the UK so far comes from a 'thinkpiece' commissioned by the National College for Leadership of Schools and Children's Services:

> Should schools be in the business of reflecting back to young people the contemporary paradigm of progress – in terms of values, material aspirations, consumerist behaviours – that has dominated people's lives since the middle of the last century? Or should they be actively preparing them for the very different world that awaits them and will be asking very different things of them? …The answer must be that we aspire to a time when all schools are microcosms of the world as it will need to be in 2025, that is:
>
> - living exemplars of sustainable practice
> - achieving self-sufficiency in energy, generating zero waste and zero emissions
> - growing and cooking as much fresh food as possible
> - bringing the natural world back into the school and its grounds
> - promoting diversity, equality and social cohesion in the school environment
> - learning how to create an inclusive local and global community
> - learning and teaching, through the entire curriculum, that reflects this and prepares pupils for the challenges of the future.
>
> (Porritt *et al.*, 2009).

Ideas for teaching
1. Developing a futures perspective: key concepts

STATE OF THE WORLD

The state of the world continues to give cause for concern. Issues to do with sustainability, wealth and poverty, peace and conflict, and human rights, all have a major local and global impact. Students need to know about the causes of such problems, how they will affect their lives now and in the future, and the action needed to help resolve them.

MANAGING CHANGE

In periods of rapid social and technological change the past cannot provide an accurate guide to the future. Anticipation and adaptability, foresight and flexibility, innovation and intuition, become increasingly essential tools for survival. Students need to develop such skills so they can become more adaptable and proactive towards change.

VIEWS OF THE FUTURE

People's views of the future may vary greatly depending, for example, on age, gender, class and culture, as well as their attitudes to change, the environment and technology. Students need to be aware of how views of the future differ and the ways in which this affects people's priorities in the present.

ALTERNATIVE FUTURES

At any point in time a range of different futures is possible. It is useful to distinguish between probable futures, those which seem *likely* to come about, and preferable futures, those one feels *should* come about. Students need to explore a range of probable and preferable futures, from the personal and local to the global.

HOPES AND FEARS

Hopes and fears for the future influence decision-making in the present. Fears can lead to the avoidance of problems rather than their resolution. Clarifying hopes for the future can enhance motivation in the present and positive action for change. Students need to explore their own hopes and fears for the future and learn to work creatively with them.

PAST/PRESENT/FUTURE

Interdependence exists across both space and time. We are directly linked back in time by the oldest members of the community and forward nearly a century by those born today. Students need to explore these links and gain a sense of both continuity and change as well as of responsibility for the future.

VISIONS FOR THE FUTURE

The first decades of a new century provide a valuable opportunity for reviewing the state of society. What needs to be left behind and what taken forward? In particular, what visions of a better future are needed to motivate active and responsible citizenship in the present? Students need to develop their skills of envisioning and of creative imagination.

FUTURE GENERATIONS

Economists, philosophers and international lawyers increasingly recognise the rights of future generations. It has been suggested that no generation should inherit less human and natural wealth than the one that preceded it. Students need to discuss the rights of future generations and what the responsibility to uphold these may involve.

SUSTAINABLE FUTURES

Current consumerist lifestyles are increasingly seen as unsustainable. A sustainable society would prioritize concern for the environment, for the poorest members of the community, and for the needs of future generations. Students need to understand how this applies to their everyday lives and possible future employment.

Hicks (2012c)

Two classroom activities are described below. Each can be used to enhance ongoing studies of a locality and a social or environmental issue. They can be amended to suit appropriate age levels and contexts.

2. Identifying hopes and concerns

When learning about any aspect of local or global society it is important to explore learners' hopes and concerns about the issue being studied. Not to do so is to ignore the affective domain (*see* Chapter 5) and its centrality to learning. The teacher's task here is threefold: to ensure that learners really feel they are being listened to; to explore relevant examples of positive action for change occurring locally and globally; and to explore action for change initiated by young people locally and globally.

Supposing the focus were the local environment, natural or built, the steps could be as follows:

- Learners individually list two or three *concerns* they have about the future of the local environment and describe how these make them feel.
- These concerns are then shared in small groups with each group reporting back briefly to the whole class on two issues of their choice.
- A composite class list is then compiled under the heading 'Concerns for the future of the local environment'.
- Whole-class discussion teases out the key elements that have arisen from this process.

The same four steps should then be used to explore learners' *hopes* for the local environment. This process brings out into the open matters that are often overlooked and ignored. Just sharing hopes and concerns can help to alleviate some of the fears associated with them. As one student exclaimed: 'It's not just me then that worries about these things!'

This is only the first step. After naming concerns and hopes (which may mirror each other), learners need to explore relevant examples of action for change taken by adults and young people. In the case of the local environment this might be finding out about the work of a wildlife group in the community and carrying out activities of their own or with the group. Acknowledging the learner's fears and concerns, and then looking at case studies of working for change, can help to develop a positive and healthy sense of efficacy and agency, and this lies at the heart of local and global citizenship.

3. Probable/preferable futures

It is useful to think first about probable futures because these are the futures we are most likely to have to deal with. This could be in relation to one's personal future, the local future, e.g. the prospect that traffic congestion will get worse, or the global future, e.g. that climate change will mean more floods and more droughts. Local government, town planners, business and industry are all constantly planning for probable futures – although this does not mean that people necessarily agree on what the future will be like.

Politicians, non-governmental organizations, town planners, business and industry are also concerned with preferable futures. They have a vision of what the future ought to be like and they work towards achieving it –

but this doesn't mean people necessarily agree on what the preferable future should be like.

Given the focus of this book on climate change, peak oil and the limits to growth as elements of the probable future, the preferable future needs to be a low or post-carbon future of some sort. How this might be achieved and what it might look like is the subject of the following chapters.

Five things a school can do

- Staff need to become more knowledgeable about futures thinking via www.teaching4abetterworld.co.uk/docs/download18.pdf (Chapter 2).
- Time needs to be set aside for staff to share their own feelings about the need for clearer futures thinking and to discuss the implications for school policy and practice.
- Every school should include in its policy documents a statement on the need for learners to develop a futures perspective in relation to their own lives and the local and global community.
- Awareness of futures thinking should be introduced into curriculum and practice so that it becomes the norm for both children and teachers.
- Such work should include envisioning of the future (*see* Chapter 9) and be central to all learning for sustainability.

Chapter 6
Accepting transition

What transition?

Climate change, the end of easy oil and the limits to growth will all have a significant and major impact on the future. Each is subject to ideological controversy and debate, yet we have reached the time when appropriate action for change needs to be taken at individual, local, national and global levels. This marks the beginning of a social, cultural, economic and environmental transition that will last for a considerable time. We can be sure about this – because the effects of climate change on both humans and the biosphere will be felt for centuries; because we have left behind the century in which oil was easily available on a vast scale; and because, whether we accept or deny the ecological limits to growth the consequences will be long lasting.

The scientific evidence suggests that the effects of climate change will be felt for generations to come (Archer, 2009). The impacts will vary depending on where one lives in the world and one's socioeconomic status. In the UK we are experiencing unseasonal weather, storm surges, flash flooding, water shortages, drought and warming temperatures. Climate change will affect every aspect of daily life – what we eat and where it comes from, our gardens, our leisure pursuits and our work patterns. Farming, business, industry, transport, health and housing will all need to be radically rethought.

Opinion differs on when peak oil production might actually peak, but the availability of easy oil will decline during the course of the twenty-first century (ASPO, 2013). Oil will not *suddenly* disappear, but it will become more costly to get and require more energy to produce. Given the record of the oil industry, drilling in new fragile locations such as the Arctic, which is already changing rapidly because of global warming, may cause major environmental damage. Similarly the use of 'fracking', which seems to open up new opportunities for shale gas, is likely to stay mired in controversy (Heinberg, 2013). Our energy and transport futures are increasingly uncertain and the continuing burning of oil and coal will only add to global warming.

The predominant neoliberal worldview, which drives free-market economics, sees no limits to growth and views problems that may arise as solvable by technological breakthroughs and human ingenuity. Yet major water shortages are already predicted in various parts of the world, marine ecosystems are threatened, resource wars are likely, and rich-world consumerism is beginning to hiccup seriously in the face of financial disaster and the greed of investment bankers. The limits to growth have already been surpassed – as ecological overshoot day occurs earlier each year.

However, one may say we have been here before. Dire warnings about the likelihood of future disasters are as old as history. In the twentieth century the world survived World War Two, and the subsequent Cold War did not result in nuclear annihilation. We have not recently been hit by an asteroid. It is also true that we have a penchant for disaster movies, so there is certainly something in the human psyche that circles round alarming possibilities. In reality, millions of people experience the apocalypse of war, famine, violence and torture. This world *is* a disturbing place to live in, but not everyone suffers at the same time nor is the suffering equally distributed. We are faced with the dilemma of how to be present to the pain of others and yet to continue caringly with our own lives.

The reasons for current denial about these troubled times and about the necessary transition that lies ahead is that it confronts us with our deepest human fears. Denial can take the form of feeling one doesn't need to know about troubling matters. The ways in which we avoid considering the future feed into this anxiety. Joanna Macy argues that pain for the world is precisely what marks these current times:

> To be conscious in our world today is to be aware of vast suffering and unprecedented peril. Even the words – fear, anger, sorrow – are inadequate to convey the feelings we experience, for these connote emotions long familiar to our species. The feelings that assail us now cannot be equated with ancient dreads of mortality and the 'heartache and the thousand natural shocks that flesh is heir to'. Their source lies less in concerns for the personal self than in apprehension of collective suffering – of what happens to our own and other species, to the legacy of our ancestors, to unborn generations, and to the living body of the Earth.
>
> (Macy and Brown, 1998: 27)

The problem, says Macy, is not with our pain for the world but in our repression of it. The purpose of pain is to send a warning signal that remedial action is needed. Macy cites the psychological sources of repression: the fear of pain, fear of despair, fear of appearing morbid, distrust of our own intelligence, fear of causing distress, fear of appearing weak and emotional, fear of being unpatriotic.

The fact that the future might involve major changes in lifestyle goes against everything the rich world believes in. It feels impossible because we believe 'history doesn't work in that way' and, anyway, there is always progress over time. These are core beliefs, deeply embedded in the culture and worldview of the Western world. But on a long timescale that is not necessarily true. A growing number of writers have begun to address the issue of what transition on such a scale might involve. Diamond (2006) has reviewed the history of past societies and identified five factors that lead to either collapse or success. They are: the human impact on the environment; climate change, both natural and man-induced; enemies, i.e. hostile neighbours; friends, i.e. supportive neighbours; and the effectiveness of societies' institutional responses to threats. Diamond notes that although modern society is very different from the past, some of these differences make today's society even more prone to collapse.

Who is leading denial of the inevitability of the coming transition? The answer lies in differing political ideologies or worldviews (*see* the Introduction). Politics in its widest sense is about issues of power and authority at all levels of society, from the individual and family to organizations and the state. Who has authority and what do they have authority to do? How did they gain this authority and how do they use it? What view do they have of human relationships and community? Going back to the definition of ideology given in the first chapter, it is clear that one person's truth can be seen by another as their error or denial.

Since the neoliberal view of free-market economics rests on the notion of endless growth and a competitive market, it is the prime candidate for a 'business as usual' view of the future. However, after the financial crash of 2008 and the subsequent global recession political commentators are beginning to seriously question the assumption of never-ending growth.

> The true problem is that the framework in which economic policy is cast is 100 per cent wrong. At the heart of this calamitous strategy is a wholesale misdiagnosis of how the market economy functions and a complete failure to understand why the financial crisis took place, the profundity of its impact and its implications for policy. For a generation, business and finance, cheered on by US neoconservatives and free market fundamentalists, have argued that the less capitalism is governed, regulated and shaped by the state, the better it works. Markets do everything best – managing business and systemic risk, innovating, investing, organizing executive reward – without the intervention of the supposed dead

hand of the state and without any acknowledgement of wider social obligations. The lesson of the financial crisis is that this is complete hokum that serves the political and personal interests of the very rich.

(The Observer, 20.05.2012)

The 'hokum' explains why the dangers of environmental pollution, acid rain, the ozone hole, smoking and global warming have been denied by powerful right-wing interest groups (Oreskes and Conway, 2010; Mann, 2012). There is a political fight yet to emerge over whether society does face a major social, economic and cultural transition or not.

What then might be some of the features of this coming transition? Richard Heinberg's *The Party's Over* (2005) argues that the world is about to change dramatically as a result of the depletion of 'easy' oil. He explores how the availability of abundant cheap oil in the twentieth century encouraged economic and industrial growth on a scale never before seen. The decline of conventional oil reserves and the problems associated with non-conventional oil production, despite the availability of coal, will compel us to live in a much leaner energy future. Since climate change demands a zero carbon future the transition will be one of 'energy descent', i.e. we will have less energy to use than we did before.

In *Future Scenarios* (2009), David Holmgren looks at the combined effects of peak oil and climate change and suggests four possible 'energy descent' scenarios, depending on whether climate change is mild or severe and whether oil decline is fast or slow. His four scenarios are: *Brown Tech* (slow oil decline and fast climate change), *Green Tech* (slow oil decline and slow climate change), *Earth Steward* (fast oil decline and slow climate change) and *Lifeboats* (fast oil decline and fast climate change). Such scenarios are not predictions about the future but rather attempts to analyse possible consequences of climate change and peak oil. Although varying in their impact globally, all four scenarios would result in major social, environmental and economic changes in lifestyle. A neoliberal view would see Holmgren's analysis as unduly pessimistic and as underestimating the human capacity for ingenuity and technological innovation.

How difficult might life become? As an admirer of David Orr's work I was interested to see what he would say in *Down to the Wire: Confronting climate collapse* (2009). I was shocked to find that, rather than talking about a 'long transition' he speaks of a 'long emergency'. At root he sees humanity as a species still in its adolescence and therefore lacking the experience and wisdom needed for its survival. For two centuries, he argues, we have been on a collision course with the limits of the earth and there is no historical precedent for what we now have to face. The challenges ahead, he suggests, will be more difficult than we have been led to believe and will lead to severe social, economic and political trauma. It will take stamina and vision for humanity to survive the transition he envisages.

Acknowledging transition

What does it mean to acknowledge transition? First, it means being open to the possibility that society faces a major cultural transition. Second, it's about wanting to find out more. Third, it is accepting the real possibility of such a shift occurring. Fourth, it is about joining with others to prepare for such a changed future. Various researchers and commentators are now writing about the 'long transition' (Kunstler, 2006; McKibben, 2010; Heinberg and Lerch, 2010; Martenson, 2011) because they believe that such information needs to be made more widely available and that being forewarned is forearmed. Human beings are able to respond to potential and actual adversity in extraordinary ways, and therein lies hope. The preceding chapters have given examples of the ways in which problems are being faced and alternatives acted on. In this sense the news is good.

An active and growing community response to these issues has emerged and is growing – the Transition Network. This is one of the numerous local–global initiatives to combat unsustainable practice and create a more sustainable future, but it is a particularly pertinent one. The idea was born in 2004, when Rob Hopkins (2013) was pondering what could be done about issues of climate change and peak oil. Inherent within the problems he saw were also enormous opportunities. What would happen if a number of people in each community came together to see what could be done locally about climate change and peak oil? What would that look like in practice, on the ground? From 35 transition initiatives in 2008, when the *Transition Handbook* was published (Hopkins, 2008), the number had risen to over 2,000 in more than 35 countries by 2012 (Transition Network, 2013). In *The Transition Companion* (2011) Hopkins sets out the principles, procedures and practices of this prescient initiative.

It begins with a small number of people in a community identifying a shared concern about climate change and peak oil. A local group is formed and members identify the interest groups they wish to set up. These generally focus on energy, transport, food, building and housing, health and well-being, although all Transition initiatives have their own unique stamp. Gradually the initial group works to include as diverse a population as possible, drawing in as many sectors of the local community as it can. A key tool in forward planning is the use of visioning (*see* Chapter 8) to identify what the key elements of a local post-carbon future need to be.

Other concepts central to the Transition Movement are local resilience and 'energy descent' plans. The idea that we need to rebuild local resilience in the face of turbulent times is increasingly gaining ground (Newman *et al.*, 2009) and has become a fundamental tenet of the Transition Network. In times past, communities were often more reliant than they are today on local sources of food and energy – indeed geography made them so. A community that can provide many of its needs from the local area is infinitely more resilient than one that depends on worldwide networks for its provision. In a stable world this is not a problem, but with a long and edgy transition in prospect local resilience takes on new importance. The consequent aim is to draw up an Energy Descent Action Plan, a comprehensive document that studies every aspect of local energy use and how it can be reduced, based on zero-carbon technologies.

Experience over time has shown that the Transition process generally goes through five main stages, as described in Box 6.1.

Box 6.1 – Transition initiatives: five stages

The process goes from meeting other interested people and deciding to try Transition ('Starting Out'), to becoming a viable project ('Deepening'), then broadening engagement with the local community ('Connecting') and scaling things up to make localization a reality ('Building'). Lastly, there is a visionary stage of reflecting on what Transition would look like were it to happen more widely ('Daring to Dream').

1. Starting Out

This stage begins with Transition as an aspiration and progresses to getting it under way with a good chance of success. Some of the key ingredients at this stage are coming together as a group, exploring inclusion and diversity, using respectful communication, awareness raising, envisioning the future, forming working groups and building partnerships.

---

2. DEEPENING

The initiative will build momentum and practical projects will emerge. The work will need to be deepened, broadening engagement across the community, being more efficient and effective. This includes exploring how the group communicates, celebrating important moments, relearning old/lost skills, keeping the momentum up, creating local food initiatives, developing personal resilience.

3. CONNECTING

It is often said that a full-scale response to peak oil and climate change would be akin to the preparations for World War Two. The ingredients now focus on how things can be taken to a wider audience. This includes involving the local council, working with local businesses, collecting oral histories, engaging young people, using the skills of storytelling.

4. BUILDING

Transition groups aim ultimately to catalyse the localization of their local economy. This will lead to the development of social enterprises, e.g. banks, energy companies and so on. Ingredients include energy descent action plans, scaling up the group's impact, developing strategic local infrastructure, intermediate technologies and community ownership of assets.

5. DARING TO DREAM

The ingredients in this stage involve the stepping up of Transition thinking to the national stage – imagining what it might look like if every settlement had vibrant Transition initiatives, setting up food networks, energy companies, growing food everywhere, catalysing a new national culture of social enterprise.

Source: Summarized from:
www.transitionnetwork.org/ingredients

The report from Taunton Transition Town (*see* Box 6.2), gives a snapshot of the way in which some Transition initiatives are beginning to work with their local council to promote greater local resilience. This is a good example of change occurring democratically, from the bottom up rather than top down.

Box 6.2 - Case study: Transition in action

Towards a resilient Taunton Deane – from then to now
By Chrissie Godfrey

In 2009, Taunton Transition Town (TTT) ran an exemplary visioning exercise with their local borough council at the request of the council's strategic director. It brought together almost all the council's 375 employees, from senior management to plumbers, plus over half of the council's elected members, to create a vision for a post-oil Taunton Deane. They were asked to creatively get to grips with what the area needed to become resilient.

The resulting ideas were pulled together into 'Towards a Resilient Taunton Deane', a document whose story has kept the council buzzing ever since. The strategic director instantly created a Green Champions team to promote all things green across the organisation. The council joined the 10:10 campaign, and by November 2010 has achieved a saving of 9.87 per cent on its energy usage. Each department now has a Green Charter, and there are regular events to keep Transition alive for all staff. Other spin-offs include:

- A planning officer and a car park attendant independently planting a new apple orchard on public land. They didn't even know each other before our workshops.
- Our being invited to address the Local Strategic Partnership (LSP) about peak oil and resilience, resulting in their giving TTT a grant to repeat the workshops in the community. We have now run seven, and after each one pulled together the visions and ideas into a printed and illustrated story to give back to the community, highlighting local priorities and intentions.
- After one workshop in the highly rural Neroche Parish, their new parish plan now has a strong 'green' element.
- In Wellington, the workshop helped the existing transition group increase their membership and identify priorities. At least four other Transition-style groups are also emerging as a result.
- Local Transition members now work with the council's new climate change officer to recruit new volunteers to act as Home Energy Auditor. Ten of these, all trained to NVQ standards, provide free advice to householders on cutting bills.

Source: Hopkins (2011: 115)

The UK's first comprehensive Energy Descent Action Plan, *Transition in Action* (Hodgson and Hopkins, 2010), explores in detail how Totnes in Devon and its district can make the post-carbon transition. Totnes was the first transition town in the UK and has developed a fund of experience and expertise in all aspects of transition. More than 500 people contributed to the detailed plan.

> The Plan explores the nuts-and-bolts practicalities of relocalising the economy of the area. It argues that in a world of highly volatile oil prices, the need for stringent cuts in carbon emissions and economic uncertainty, the globalized economy upon which we are so dependent can no longer be relied upon. Indeed it leaves us highly vulnerable. At the moment Totnes and its surrounding parishes act like a large leaky bucket. Money pours into the area through wages, grants, pensions, funding, tourist revenues and so on. In our current economic model, most of it pours back out again, and its ability to make things happen locally is lost. Each time we pay our energy bill, that money leaves the area. Each time we shop in a supermarket, 80% of that money leaves the area. Every time we shop online, that money that could have bolstered our economy leaves the area. All the while pressure grows on our local shops and businesses ... Localisation is a powerful concept. Clearly Totnes cannot become self-sufficient, nor would it want to be. It will never be able to make computers or frying pans. However, as the oral history section of this report shows, it used to be far more self-reliant than it is today, functioning far more like a bucket than its present day leaky sieve.
>
> (Hodgson and Hopkins, 2010: 13)

At the heart of the report is a vision of how Totnes and district could be in 2030, as well as a timeline showing when specific changes need to occur. After setting the scene in some detail the substance of the report covers:

- food production and farming, food security, health and well-being, water matters and ways to support biodiversity
- energy security, energy budget, transport, building and housing
- economics and livelihoods, consumption and waste
- arts, culture, media and innovation, education awareness
- local governance and community matters.

It is a model of what an Energy Descent Action Plan needs to be, looking back to the past, focusing on the present and envisioning the detail of a post-carbon future for the local community.

The overall task can be nothing less than the creation of a more sustainable future despite, or because of, the hazards that lie ahead. Jurgen Randers writes:

> The transition to sustainability will require fundamental change to a number of the systems that govern current world developments. Not only will the energy system need to change from fossil to solar, and the ruling paradigm from perpetual physical growth to some form of stability that fits within the physical carrying capacity of the globe, but there will also be changes to the softer institutional guides like capitalism, democracy, agreed power sharing, and the human perspective on nature.
>
> (Randers, 2012: 13)

When the Transition Network started, it was framed as a response to climate change and peak oil but, as the network has spread globally, a range of further reasons have emerged for people getting involved. These include 'because it feels more fun than not doing it', 'because of wanting a fairer world', 'because it means people can do the project they've always wanted', 'because it feels like the most appropriate thing to do' and 'because it gives me hope' (Hopkins, 2011).

The role of education

So what should be the role of education in preparing young people for such a social, cultural and economic transition? These questions take us back to the educational territory explored in the Introduction. The UK has a long tradition in education that stresses the need for pupils and students to understand both self and society. Education in the face of transition will sharpen this aim and be of theoretical and practical use for the future. Right-wing educationalists may cry 'indoctrination!', since some scent danger if teachers suggest all is not be well with society. At the time of writing, the Conservative/Liberal Democrat Coalition was in the process of reducing the National Curriculum, in theory leaving schools free to decide for themselves some of what they might wish to teach.

The introduction referred to the Sustainable Schools programme, which existed under the previous Labour government, and some of its exemplar documents sidelined after the 2010 General Election. However, in 2013 education for sustainable development still had official educational backing in the UK, and Schools Minister Lord Hill officially launched the new Sustainable Schools Alliance that year, saying: 'Sustainability issues are an increasingly important part of our everyday life. That's why I welcome the new Sustainable Schools Alliance, which will help make these issues an increasingly important part of school life.' The role of the Alliance is described as follows:

> Schools make a vital contribution to sustainable development. By reducing their carbon emissions they protect the environment and save money. By encouraging learning and practical action about sustainability amongst pupils they foster sustainable behaviours in young people that will remain with them throughout their lives. By operating at the heart of communities they can foster social cohesion and sustainable behaviours throughout the local area.
>
> (Sustainable Schools Alliance, 2013)

The Alliance provides a first port of call for schools looking for advice and support on education for sustainability. It aims to draw together evidence for the benefits of such education as part of its support for schools.

Sustainability and Environmental Education (SEEd) (2013), one of the major bodies involved in the creation of the Alliance, promotes environmental education and education for sustainable development (ESD) in the UK. Its services include: training and capacity building, ESD pedagogy and curriculum, supporting Sustainable Schools, facilitation and consultancy. Its recent initiative, to identify and elaborate the parameters for a Sustainability Curriculum, has had wide support.

It is vital to have educational materials available that prepare students for the changing circumstances of the twenty-first century. Currently, few educational resources are suggesting that the future our children inherit will be very different from the present or that a zero carbon society will demand significant lifestyle changes. The Transition Network is a vital resource for schools in demonstrating active citizenship at local levels in all sorts of inspiring ways (Hicks, 2008). Schools can learn from local and national examples of transition initiatives and can also contribute much to them, building a new strand in school–community relationships.

Ideas for teaching
1. Key transition issues
Since climate change and peak oil are two of the key issues for the Transition Network, the ideas for teaching suggested in Chapters 1 and 2 can be used to illustrate the concerns with which transition initiatives are involved around the world.

2. Using future scenarios

One way of helping young people think more critically and creatively about transition is through the use of scenarios. In the example given in Figure 6.1, an activity taken from *Sustainable Schools, Sustainable Futures* (Hicks, 2012a), pupils are asked to reflect on what local well-being might look like in a more sustainable future, as part of a wider scheme of work on the topic. The purpose of this activity is for pupils to explore, debate and discuss this scenario for sustainable local well-being.

Figure 6.1: What might local sustainable well-being look like?
Reproduced with permission of World Wide Fund for Nature UK

Each pupil will need a copy of the scenario and the accompanying questions.

- Brief the class on the purpose and use of scenarios (*see* Chapter 9) and go through the five questions below that need to be answered.
- Pupils work in small groups. First they individually note down their own responses to the questions below and then work to create composite small group responses.
- Groups then take it in turns to share their response with the rest of the class. Either the group responses or a composite class response to each question is put up for display.

Scenario questions

Look carefully at the scenario of what local well-being might look like in a more sustainable future. Imagine you are visiting this future with a group of friends to gather information about it. You can look around to see how things are different and listen to what people are saying about life in this future.

1. What are people doing and saying that is different?

2. What are the advantages of living in this future?

3. What questions do you have about this future?

3. A-level Transition

Recently the Transition Network was approached by one of the UK examination boards requesting permission for an exam question on transition to appear in their Citizenship Studies A-level examination. Kevin Walker, a citizenship teacher, sent the following account to the Transition Network.

> This summer's A-level exam papers in England, Wales & Northern Ireland included questions on the Transition Movement. The Global Citizen unit of the A-level in Citizenship Studies included two questions, the first focused on the applicability of the Transition model to the student's own community and the second asked the student to consider the relative global impact of community based initiatives in contrast to governmental actions.
>
> Students were informed in advance of the topic area but not the specific questions so they had a chance to research the topic beforehand. Their answers demonstrated a genuine concern regarding the impact of climate change and some knowledge of the concept of peak oil but most knew little about the Transition Movement until they undertook their research. This often revealed

local initiatives of which they were generally unaware and in a few cases it led onto their own involvement. In all cases these 17–18 year olds engaged critically with the issues and reflected deeply on the role of the active global citizens which they are becoming.

(Walker, 2012)

In educating for transition, teachers and their pupils will be breaking new ground and that ground will require careful watering and special nourishment.

4. Schools in Transition

The Schools in Transition programme is a new initiative for schools interested in becoming involved in transition in, and with, their local communities. Further details can be found at www.transitionnetwork.org/support/education/schools-transition

Five things a school can do

- Staff need to become more knowledgeable about the work of the Transition Network through its website: www.transitionnetwork.org
- Time needs to be set aside for staff to share their own responses to transition initiatives and to discuss how they could contribute to school policy and practice.
- Every school should include in its policy documents a statement about the need for a zero carbon future and the ways in which it is working towards this.
- Awareness of/engagement with Transition initiatives should be introduced into curriculum and practice, and become the norm for children and teachers.
- Schools engaged in sustainability education should recognize that they have much to contribute to local Transition initiatives.

Part Three

Sources of hope

3

Taking wind speed readings at St Columb Minor School

Chapter 7
The nature of hope

Hope and despair

For any dilemma or problem we bring to children's attention we also need to explore with them ways in which others are responding positively to the challenges it presents. Otherwise, we can unwittingly evoke despair. I know from many years' teaching about global issues that pupils and students respond to information about the state of the world in different ways. Some feel excited or challenged, wanting to know more; others feel worried or even overwhelmed. Some students challenge the veracity of the information they are exploring; others feel it is exaggerated and go into denial. This made me wonder how educators who had to teach about, or work with, painful global issues on a daily basis managed to stay cheerful. What kept them going?

Part of the answer, I realized, was hope – not 'shallow' hope, but 'deep hope' to tap into in troubled times when major changes loom ahead. The opposite of hope is despair, so we need to consider this powerful feeling too. We may experience despair when something goes seriously wrong in our lives – when a friend has a terminal illness, when someone is imprisoned unjustly, when a child dies; or when we realize that global warming is here to stay. But even in the most difficult circumstances people find ways of confronting such despair so that they can continue to function and act. Despair can lead to the discovery of previously unknown resources in oneself, which can be drawn on. Despair has a useful function: it may feel like the end of the road, utter numbness or death, yet it can lead us to summon powers we didn't know we had.

Despair, therefore, has its hopeful aspects. Psychologist James Hillman points out that deep despair can actually feel like death, but that it can nevertheless contain within it the seeds of a way forward. He writes: 'Despair ushers in the death experience and is at the same time the requirement for resurrection. Life as it was before, the *status quo ante*, died when despair was born. There is only the moment as it is – the seed of whatever may come' (Hillman, 1978: 93). Despair thus has a pivotal role to play in psychological transformation. At that moment, Hillman points out, there is no hope but it is in that dark place that transformation can begin. Theologian Jurgen Moltmann puts it slightly differently: 'Despair is the premature, arbitrary anticipation of the non-fulfilment of what we hope for from God ... the pain of despair surely lies in the fact that a hope is there, but no way opens up for its fulfilment' (1967: 23). So although hope can thus arise from despair, we do not necessarily have to consciously visit that traumatized place in order to become aware of our deepest hopes and yearnings.

The importance of hope

Why is hope so central to the human condition? Futurist Wendell Bell argues:

> The human condition is ... constituted in hope. The meanings of our lives depend importantly on our visions of the future. Without the possibility of a future, there is nothing left but despair. Thus, if we give up the future, we give up on ourselves. The ancient prophecy remains true: Where there is no vision the people perish. One reason, then, why the present generation ought to be concerned about the well-being of future generations is that the continuation of humanity is necessary for present hope.
>
> (Bell, 1993: 81)

One of the reasons why hope and despair were so present during the superpower nuclear arms race (1949–89) was because the future of humanity itself was threatened. For a species to become extinct is the end of hope. That we find ourselves part of an unwished-for global experiment in transition, the outcome of which is unclear, can also be grounds for despair.

Paolo Freire, in his exploration of social justice and education, *Pedagogy of Hope*, writes:

> While I certainly cannot ignore hopelessness as a concrete entity, nor turn a blind eye to the historical, economic and social reasons that explain that hopelessness – I do not understand human existence, and the struggle needed to improve it, apart from hope and dream. Hope is an ontological need. Hopelessness is but hope that has lost its bearings, and become a distortion of that ontological need ... Without a minimum of hope, we cannot so much as start the struggle. But without the struggle, hope, as an ontological need, dissipates, loses its bearings, and turns into hopelessness. And hopelessness can become tragic despair. Hence the need for a kind of education in hope.
>
> (Freire, 2004: 2–3)

Two things strike me. First is the description of hope as an ontological need, something that is part of the essence of human nature. Second, the need for some kind of 'education in hope'. Educator Robin Richardson explores the relationship between hope and story like this:

> Today, then, myths of hope. The grand narrative of hope was succinctly summarised by Dennis Potter. 'No matter how corrupt, wicked, cruel, disastrous, the world is, some little tributary of feeling says it's all right' – 'That is where,' he continued, 'the writing comes from'. He might have said where the myths come from. That is what myths are for. Hope that 'it's all right' is kept alive in story and imagery: 'The wolf shall dwell with the lamb, and the leopard shall lie down with the kid. The calf and the lion cub together, with a little child to lead them. They shall not hurt or destroy ...'. The myth that peace is possible, or if not possible anyway worth fighting for.
>
> (Richardson, 1996: 70)

Richardson goes on:

> We need stories – myths and folktales as well as true accounts – to help us hold the beginnings, middles and ends of our lives together. Without them we shall not have hope: yes, to lose stories is to lose hope, but conversely to construct and cherish stories is to maintain hope ... And [as] Italo Calvino says ... 'The ultimate meaning to which all stories refer has two faces: the continuity of life, the inevitability of death'.
>
> (ibid.: 101–2)

The last sentence echoes the words of James Hillman and others who have pointed out that, at heart, issues of hope and despair relate to and echo the continuity of life and the inevitability of death. This is what much of myth and story is essentially about – beginnings and endings, the mysteries of the human condition.

Jurgen Moltmann provides some of the deepest insights into the nature of hope, and given the tasks that lie ahead I believe we need to acquaint ourselves with some of those depths, for they essentially relate to what it means to be human.

> Hope alone is to be called 'realistic', because it alone takes seriously the possibilities with which reality is fraught. It does not take things as they happen to stand or lie, but as progressing, moving things with possibilities of change ... Thus hopes and anticipations of the future are not a transfiguring glow superimposed upon a

darkened existence, but are realistic ways of perceiving the scope of our real possibilities, and as such they set everything in motion and keep it in a state of change. Hope and the kind of thinking that goes with it consequently cannot submit to the reproach of being utopian, for they do not strive after things that have 'no place', but after things that have 'no place *as yet*' but can acquire one.

(Moltmann, 1967: 25)

In a later work Moltmann writes:

Whoever begins with hope is aiming to create new experiences. Hope does not guarantee that one will have the wished-for experiences. Life in hope entails risk and leads one into danger and confirmation, disappointment and surprise. We must therefore speak of the *experiment of hope* ... In the experiment of hope the object at stake is always one's own life ... Hope must therefore be sufficiently comprehensive and profound. It must encompass happiness and pain, love and mourning, life and death if it is not to lead us into illusion.

(Ibid., 1975: 188–9)

Given the scope of the task before us as educators, these words may sustain us in the days ahead. Few educators or academics talk about hope, but it is essential to the task we face in the approaching transition, both for those we teach and those who come after.

One of the few educators who, like Freire, has grasped the significance of hope is the environmental educator David Orr. It was Orr's *Down to the Wire: Confronting climate collapse* (2009) that alerted me to the responsibilities that educators have. He puts his finger precisely on the dilemma of education for transition when he says: 'Radical hope anticipates a good for which those who have the hope as yet lack the appropriate concepts with which to understand it' (ibid.: 173). He quotes theologian Reinhold Niebuhr's words:

Nothing that is worth doing can be achieved in a lifetime; therefore we must be saved by hope. Nothing which is true or beautiful or good makes complete sense in any immediate context of history; therefore we must be saved by faith. Nothing we do, however virtuous, can be accomplished alone; therefore, we are saved by love. No virtuous act is quite as virtuous from the standpoint of our friend or foe as it is from our standpoint. Therefore we must be saved by the final form of love which is forgiveness.

(Niebuhr, quoted by Orr, 2009: 181)

And less we confuse optimism with hope, Orr explains:

> Realistic hope, however, requires us to check our optimism at the door and enter the future without illusions. It requires a level of honesty, self-awareness, and sobriety that is difficult to summon and maintain. I know a great many smart people and many very good people, but I know far fewer people who can handle hard truth gracefully without despairing ... Authentic hope, in other words, is made of sterner stuff than optimism. It must be rooted in the truth as best we can see it, knowing that our vision is always partial. Hope requires the courage to reach farther, dig deeper, confront our limits and those of nature, and work harder. Optimism doesn't have to work very hard, since it is likely to win anyway, but hope has to hustle, scheme, make deals, and strategize.

(Ibid.: 185)

My initial exploration of the nature of hope some years ago felt like a turning point in my life. In the endless quest for positive ways forward it felt as if I had at last dug deep enough to touch against something of great worth. That worth felt twofold: first in the quality of thinking demonstrated by these 'explorers of life' and, second in the deep connection of their subject matter to the human condition.

Sometimes life backs up such insights in mundane but unlikely ways. While holidaying on the Dorset coast one summer I happened to notice a Latin tag on the label of the beer bottle I was holding, '*Dum spiro spero*' – 'While there's life, there's hope.' This squared the circle for me, as my childhood hero, space pilot Dan Dare in the *Eagle* comic, had uttered those very words when all seemed lost on an alien planet. I didn't know then that this was an ancient Latin saying, but I sensed that the words meant something really important that I couldn't yet fathom.

Sources of hope

Given the role of hope in troubled times it is vital to identify the sources of hope that educators and others can draw on. Before I began to explore this I had no notions of what those sources might be, even for myself. Whatever the sources were, they did not seem willing to reveal themselves easily; they felt occluded somewhere in my psyche. I decided therefore to explore the experiences of educators who regularly taught about global issues to see how they managed to retain a sense of hope and optimism. The research took place over the course of a residential weekend, and participants were asked to keep a reflective journal recording their thoughts and feelings as they engaged with the question of hope (Hicks, 2006b). In initial discussion about the state of the world they named issues such as continuing damage to the planet, abuse of human rights, hunger and poverty, racism, and the power of multinational corporations. Professionally they felt stressed, overworked and marginalized, and when prompted to identify the feelings that went with this they spoke about anger, indignation, frustration and despair. They didn't find it easy to acknowledge these feelings – wanting to deny the discomfort of the affect – but were prepared to admit that this was the context within which any notion of hope had to be set. As they began to share their writing and their experiences the work became deeper. Towards the end of the weekend participants were asked to draw together the collective sources of hope they felt they had identified. The results are shown in Box 7.1.

> ## Box 7.1 – Sources of hope
> - *The natural world* ~ a source of beauty, wonder and inspiration which ever renews itself and ever refreshes the heart and mind.
> - *Other people's lives* ~ the way in which both ordinary and extraordinary people manage difficult life situations with dignity.
> - *Collective struggles* ~ groups in the past and the present which have fought to achieve the equality and justice that is rightfully theirs.
> - *Visionaries* ~ those who offer visions of an earth transformed and who work to help bring this about in different ways.
> - *Faith and belief* ~ which may be spiritual or political and which offers a framework of meaning in both good times and bad.
> - *A sense of self* ~ being aware of one's self-worth and secure in one's own identity which leads to a sense of connectedness and belonging.
> - *Human creativity* ~ the constant awe-inspiring upwelling of music, poetry, and the arts, an essential element of the human condition.
> - *Mentors and colleagues* ~ at work and at home who offer inspiration by their deeds and encouragement with their words.
> - *Relationships* ~ the being loved by partners, friends and family that nourishes and sustains us in our lives.

> - *Humour* ~ seeing the funny side of things, being able to laugh in adversity, having fun, celebrating together.
> - *Roots* ~ links with the past, childhood, history, previous generations, ancestors, the need to honour continuity.
> - *Human creativity* ~ both individual and community, music, song and dance, painting and sculpture, books, stories, poetry, utopia.
>
> *Source*: Hicks, D. (2006b)

I was awed by the results of this shared experience. On the one hand the results felt a revelation, yet part of me said: 'Yes, of course!' The answers had not come easily to the participants, who had come knowing that there was something there for them but were unsure what it might be. They came knowing that hope was clearly important, but were unsure exactly how. What once was a somewhat nebulous feeling was revealed to be at the heart of the human experience and deeply rooted in the powerful life-experiences of each person.

The participants were asked to bring to the weekend an item that was in some way a symbol of hope for them, and each person spoke about what they had brought. The items included photos of family and friends, a piece of music, a picture, natural objects, a book, and various artefacts and gifts. One by one these items were placed in the centre of the circle. A deep silence followed the end of this sharing. In the closing session one participant commented that the weekend had itself been a source of hope. It was an event that engaged head and heart, the personal and professional, the past and the future. It was also ultimately of practical daily value. At the time I wrote:

> The list is a striking tribute to the resilience and resourcefulness of this group of educators. Although many of these sources of hope were previously implicit in their personal and professional lives, it was the research process itself which made them explicit, visible and therefore more available as a source of creative energy ... One of the most striking things about the ... process was that the event provided not only the richest data but it also became a source of hope in its own right. Participants said that they felt nourished, renewed, clearer about what kept them going, more aware of the 'tapestry of hope', witnesses to faith in the human spirit.
>
> (Hicks, 2006b: 74–5)

Discussion of the need for hope in troubled times is vitally important; identifying and sharing one's own sources of hope in a safe context can be even more valuable and rewarding. The fact that we don't often openly discuss such matters is because they relate to the heart and, as discussed in previous chapters, we often feel this needs protecting. But in sharing them, in a safe space, we begin to get in touch with our creative energies again.

The role of education

What I learnt from this work was that hope and despair are central to the human condition and that to enter this territory involves head, heart and soul. To try and deal with these matters solely through the intellect is a contradiction in terms. It requires a holistic and experiential approach. We know that issues to do with feelings, the future, global issues and transition are often experienced as uncomfortable and therefore to be kept at arm's length; but the work on hope shows there are many processes that allow learners to approach these matters with integrity. Here I mean education in its broadest sense and focus on adults, particularly on possibilities for teachers, tutors and trainee teachers.

Hope and despair are also deeply felt by young people as they try to grapple with contemporary global issues. Here Elin Kelsey and Carly Armstong highlight some of the problems they face:

> Climate change, the Gulf oil spill, Japan's nuclear disasters, the massive impact of Canada's tar sands – 'gloom and doom' blows in from even the most trusted places. Children and adults are confronted with environmental catastrophes almost anywhere they turn: kid-friendly nature magazines, homework assignments, popular films and ... at the zoo.
>
> (Kelsey and Armstrong, 2012: 187)

It is not only the stories in the news that are a problem, it is also how they are treated in school:

> Days and weeks can be spent in classrooms studying species extinction, climate changes, population issues, deforestation and desertification, and more ... and while teachers may be comfortable in talking about the science of species extinction, or about the geography of urban sprawl ... or about ozone holes and global climate change, the emotional implications of these subjects appear to be unexplored, and in truth, unexamined.
>
> The environmental education literature is strangely silent about dealing with the emotional implications of the environmental crisis. Words like hope, grief, mourning, sadness, despair or anger

rarely appear in our writings: there is virtually nothing in our literature addressing appropriate ways to deal with the emotions associated with environmental degradation.

(Kool and Kelsey, 2006)

This is not just a problem for environmental educators to resolve, it is a problem for all parents and educators. How do we help young people cope with, let alone manage, the complex global issues that they hear about today, issues that adults also find difficult? Causing concern, fear, even despair, among those we teach can never be an appropriate goal for education (*see* Chapter 4).

A key figure internationally in offering ways to address these issues is systems theorist and Buddhist scholar Joanna Macy. Starting with the sources of human angst and despair, she points a way forward through what she calls 'the work that reconnects'. In essence this is about reconnecting with our despair, our hopes, our visions, other like-minded people and the planet itself. While that may sound like a tall order, Macy has honed her insights and practices over fifty years to create a wealth of experiential activities to this end. These are described in *Coming Back to Life: Practices to reconnect our lives, our world* (Macy and Brown, 1998), some of which can be adapted for use with young people, and which are also explored in depth in *Active Hope* (Macy and Johnstone, 2012). The authors write:

> Active Hope is about becoming active participants in bringing about what we hope for. Active Hope is a practice. Like tai chi or gardening, it is something we *do* rather than *have*. It is a process we can apply to any situation, and it involves three key steps. First, we take a clear view of reality; second, we identify what we hope for in terms of the direction we'd like things to move in or the values we'd like to see expressed; and third, we take steps to move ourselves or our situation in that direction. Since Active Hope doesn't require our optimism, we can apply it even in areas where we feel hopeless. The guiding impetus is intention; we *choose* what we aim to bring about, act for, or express. Rather than weighing our chances and proceeding only when we feel hopeful, we focus on our intention and let it be our guide.
>
> (Macy and Johnstone, 2012: 3).

Macy and Johnstone identify three main cultural stories being enacted at present: 'Business as Usual', the 'Great Unravelling' and the 'Great Turning'. Business as Usual is the story in which many people find themselves, the consumer fantasy of free-market economics with growth and progress as their constant goals. The Great Unravelling is a story that coexists with the first, embracing economic decline, resource depletion, climate change and the mass extinction of species. The Great Turning, which is already evident, is the story of a new cultural shift, which will be as significant in its impact as the Agricultural and Industrial revolutions were:

> It's been called the Ecological Revolution, the Sustainability Revolution, even the Necessary Revolution. This is our third story: we call it the Great Turning and see it as the essential adventure of our time. It involves the transition from a doomed economy of industrial growth to a life-sustaining society committed to the recovery of our world. This transition is well under way.
>
> (ibid.: 26)

Joanna Macy (2013) describes the Great Turning as a process of empowerment which has four stages: Coming from Gratitude, Honouring our Pain for the World, Seeing with New Eyes and Going Forth. In this cycle of becoming it is possible to both experience despair and find a way forward to creative engagement with others. A flavour of these four stages and the significance of each is given below.

1. In difficult times the *practising of gratitude* can promote a sense of well-being, build trust and generosity and motivate us to act on behalf of our world. Research has shown that people experiencing high levels of gratitude tend to be more satisfied with their lives. One suggestion is to keep a gratitude journal to record at the end of the day things that have pleased us or that we feel happy about. It might be unexpectedly meeting a friend, something someone said, a beautiful sky, a small success. This practice trains us to see the good side of life as well as the bad. Coming from gratitude subtly alters our approach to life, and makes us more aware of our good fortune.

2. *Honouring our pain for the world* may at first seem impossible. A crucial response to danger, whether personal or global, is alarm and this can cause the psychology of despair to kick in. Varieties of resistance include the following: 'I don't believe it's that dangerous', 'it isn't my role to sort this out', 'I don't want to stand out from the crowd', 'this information threatens my commercial or political interests', 'it's so upsetting that I prefer not to think about it', 'I feel paralysed', 'I'm aware of the danger, but I don't know what to do' and 'there's no point in doing anything, since it won't make any difference'. We can feel caught between the pain of the way the world

appears to be going and the fear of acknowledging how bad things are, which can then trigger despair. Yet pain for the world is normal, healthy and widespread. Unlocking such blocked feelings releases energy for the journey ahead.

3. *Seeing with new eyes* can lead to a wider sense of self as we build up links over time with different communities, and with human society and the web of life itself. In the Western world we have a view of the self as separate and clearly delineated from others. This can lead to extreme individualism and narcissism. In Eastern societies the self is often seen more as part of a larger whole – family, community, society and nature – so that connections come first rather than last. We are thus all part of widening circles but may initially choose to deny it. Experiencing the wider identity that comes through interconnectedness doesn't threaten individuality but rather enhances it. Macy's Council of All Beings (1998: 149–65) demonstrates a powerful way in which non-human species can also be given a 'voice'.

4. *Going forth* is the final stage in this cycle and a consummation of all that has come before. This move into the world is about finding one's power. It is important to distinguish between old and new stories of power. The old view sees power as something that one wields over others – power *over*. Some of the consequences of this common view are that power is seen as a commodity and feelings of powerlessness are widespread, fostering mental rigidity, generating conflict and becoming suspect at all levels. The new view of power sees it instead as something to be shared – power *with*. This is a collaborative model, in which power arises from interconnectedness and creates its own synergy. Shared values, shared visions and shared purposes connect and flow through the whole. From them comes the ability to hear one's call to action and to answer it.

These four stages of empowerment are not as discrete or linear as they may appear. One moves backwards and forwards between them and cycles around them. Once committed to this sort of inner/outer process it becomes part of one's personal and professional life. Sometimes neglected, it reappears in different forms; but the call is always the same: Who am I and how am I connected to the wider whole? What am I called to do at this time?

Active Hope provides a primer for engaging actively with these times, but to enter into it requires an honesty of head, heart and soul. Yet how could anything less be sufficient for the task? Macy and Johnstone share a declaration often attributed to the poet Goethe:

Until one is committed, there is hesitancy, the chance to draw back. Concerning all acts of initiative (and creation), there is one elementary truth, the ignorance of which kills countless ideas and splendid plans: that the moment one definitely commits oneself, then Providence moves too. All sorts of things occur to help one that would never otherwise have occurred ... Whatever you can do, or dream you can do, begin it. Boldness has genius, power, and magic in it. Begin now.

(Macy and Johnstone, 2012: 200)

Joanna Macy's (2013) international work is important in these times of transition, as is Chris Johnstone's (2013) in the UK. The significance of such initiatives lies in their holistic approach, which embraces the whole person – head and heart, body and spirit – and thus reaches depths that other approaches cannot. Their websites provide details of talks, workshops and conferences for adults, and it is with adults that this work needs to start. Many of the activities in *Coming Back to Life* (Macy and Brown, 1998) can be adapted for use with young people in both formal and non-formal contexts. I trust that this present book, too, will contribute an initial thread to such a tapestry of hope.

Ideas for teaching
1. Thinking about hope
This is an activity that can be shared in circle time or small groups. Students often have a different perspective on hope from adults, because of their age. I hear them talk about parents, grandparents and other people as significant sources of inspiration and hope in their life. This is not about role models, I think, but rather about people who directly support and encourage you. It could also include people in the community or on the news who are working in different ways to create a better world.

The steps are as follows:

- One needs to begin with some observations about the importance of hope, explaining that you are not simply referring to being optimistic. When things get difficult or an issue is worrying, we often turn to friends or adults for support and encouragement, to people who can give one a sense of hope.
- Participants take it in turns in a circle or small group to briefly share an example of someone who feels like a source of hope for them and explains why this is so. They should listen respectfully to others, without interruption, until everyone has had their turn.

- Discussion can follow. Perhaps a pupil has a question relating to what someone else has said or they'd like a bit more information. After this, the teacher can ask each group to discuss whether they think these people have any qualities in common.
- The teacher should take brief summaries from each group, of who the people are, as well as their qualities, so they together create a composite list.
- This should be followed by a wider discussion about what the children have learnt from this exercise and about their sources of hope.

2. Gratitude and well-being

Gratitude is an important social emotion, which directs our warmth out to others. Gratitude has two sides: the valuing of something that has happened, and recognition of the role of someone, or something, in bringing that feeling about.

People who experience high levels of gratitude tend to feel more positive about their lives. Becoming more aware of our gratitude can lead to greater trust and cooperation with others. Here are two simple activities taken from Macy and Johnstone (2012: 44, 48–9) to enhance gratitude awareness. They can be adapted in different ways to suit different age groups.

OPEN SENTENCES

Read the following phrases that begin sentences, and see what words seem to naturally follow on from them. You can think this to yourself, or put it in writing, or try it with a partner, taking turns to speak and listen. Whenever you're not sure what to say, come back to the beginning of the sentence and see what naturally follows – it may be different each time you do this.

- Some things I love about being alive on Earth are …
- A place that was magical to me as a child was …
- My favourite activities include …
- Someone who helped me believe in myself is (or was) …
- Some things I appreciate about myself are …

GRATITUDE AWARENESS

- *Notice* – Scan your recent memories and identify something that's happened in the last 24 hours that you're pleased about. It doesn't have to be anything big, just something that makes you think 'I'm glad that happened.'

- *Savour* – Close your eyes and imagine that you are experiencing that moment again. Notice colours, tastes, sounds, smells and the sensations in your body. Notice also how you are feeling in yourself.
- *Give thanks* – Who or what helped this moment to happen? Was anyone (or anything) else involved? If so, think of them and imagine expressing your thanks.

3. Widening circles

This is an activity adapted and simplified from Macy and Brown (1996: 121), which is suitable for older students and which can be tailored to match appropriate ongoing work. 'Widening Circles' helps people to see with new eyes an issue or situation that is of major concern to them. Thus, they participate in widening circles of identity. The title comes from one of Rilke's poems, which begins: 'I live my life in widening circles/ that reach out across the world'.

Participants work in groups of four. Ask them to mentally identify an issue that concerns them. After a moment of silence, invite them to take it in turns speaking and listening to one another. Each person should briefly describe their issue from three perspectives in turn:

- from their own experience and point of view, including their feelings about the issues
- from the perspective of a person whose views are very different from their own, saying who they are when speaking as this person and using the pronoun 'I'
- from the perspective of a young person living in the future whose life will be directly affected by that particular situation.

First, though, time needs to be allowed for each person to think about the three views they are going to share. They might want to jot down a few key words to help them remember. The teacher then announces to the groups the first round, in which each person shares their own experience, allowing 4–5 minutes per person. It's best to keep an eye on the time and warn: 'You need to move on to the next person in your group in a moment or two.' Allow for moment of silence between each person and a bit longer between each of the rounds. Macy comments, 'It is a brave and generous act to make room in your mind for another's experience and to lend them your voice.' Allow time at the end for people to share how this felt in their small groups and then as a whole class.

Five things a school can do

- Ask for a volunteer to look at www.activehope.info/index.html and report back, so that interested staff can learn more about this initiative if they wish.
- If there is interest, staff might wish to participate in online training activities as part of their personal and professional development.
- Every school should help children and staff to become more aware of their own sources of hope and support, and the school itself can be a source of hope in the community.
- Schools should always distinguish between hope and optimism in their work, the latter being merely hopefulness, the former more deeply grounded.
- Schools could identify and highlight their own web of hope in the local and wider community.

Chapter 8

Sharing success stories

The importance of story

> Nobody, but nobody, was paying attention. Her arguments were sound, her ideas compelling, her phrases striking. But her speech was falling on stony ground. No one was taking any interest. She paused. 'Once upon a time,' she said, starting again. Suddenly everyone was quiet, everyone was listening.

These words open a book called *Inside Stories: Wisdom and hope for changing worlds* by Angela Wood and Robin Richardson (1992: 3). Stories have power, and stories are crucial in times of transition. *Inside Stories* celebrates the oral tradition, and the stories are arranged to suggest a sequence of fundamental experiences on the journey from birth to death. They are grouped under seven main headings corresponding to key stages of human development: *seeking* (wonderings, wanderings, quests, questions), *loving* (family, friends, lovers, partners), *challenging* (conflict, assertion, defiance, liberation), *organizing* (creating, building, managing, leading), *reflecting* (review, recollection, meanings, wisdom) and *transforming* (mortality, ending, hope, renewal).

Narrative is central to the world of story and indeed to all of human life:

> What's new? What did you do today? What have you done since we last met? In these ways, and in many others, we ask to be told stories. And in answer to such questions, we all tell stories through the day, and every day. We turn to TV and to newspapers and magazines, in order to take in stories, and to chat about them and chew on them, discuss and digest them. Much of our conversation each day, particularly our conversation with the people we are closest to and care most about, is based around stories. Human beings, it can be said, are animals who tell, listen to, discuss, dwell on, are moved by, stories.
>
> (Wood and Richardson, 1992: 23)

Stories are often about issues of wisdom and hope, so they have an important role to play in troubled times (McNaughton, 2012). In the present book you will find references to ideological stories, children's stories, cultural stories and Transition Tales. This chapter particularly focuses on the importance of true stories that illustrate successful action for change.

The first course I ever ran for student teachers was on environmental issues. I knew that too much emphasis on problems could put students off and that they needed also to explore examples of positive action for change. Accordingly, the course was in two parts: first the problems, and then the solutions. The feedback at the end of the course, however, revealed that despite the success stories, the initial problems had made them despair. This made me wonder whether I should have begun with positive stories that would engage, and only look later at the problems they help resolve.

Lisa Bardwell (1991) has explored the dilemma of presenting students with too many environmental problems and the importance of sharing success stories with them. She argues that such examples provide both the imagery and the inspiration for people to become more involved in what is going on. She stresses the implicit attractiveness of a 'good story', since stories have a beginning, a middle and an end that promises some kind of resolution or closure. She also stresses the importance of the imagery of success:

> Success stories offer imagery at two levels. First, they provide examples with which people can begin to build models of alternative approaches and the contexts in which they work ... second, a good success story includes imagery that engages one cognitively. The story need not spell out a success; often a description of a process or someone's efforts to move the system to make the difference can serve as useful positive imagery.
>
> (Bardwell, 1991: 8)

Bardwell advocates stories that are more than one-liners, and she observes that a number of success stories may be needed before students can begin to create their own alternative models of what is needed. This focus on success stories can be an important antidote to the psychology of despair.

> Positive examples, or success stories, can set a tone that provides a refreshing change from the more typical doomsday warnings or edicts for appropriate action ... If expectation can precipitate helplessness, might not exposure to the other spectrum, to examples of effective participation, enhance efficacy? Success stories hold promise in terms of helping people build more adequate models about environmental problems and their roles in addressing them. While acknowledging environmental realities, these stories establish a norm for seeing those realities as challenges ... They are

intended to help people participate, not to assure that everything is okay, or that someone else is fixing the problems.

(Ibid.: 9)

The Ashden Awards (2013) have already been cited as a rich source of success stories on the transformative impacts of renewable energy projects in schools. The stories we need to collect can be local or global and illustrate successful action in relation to different aspects of sustainability, active citizenship and transition. Stories are also needed of particular people, from the past and present, who by their words and deeds have shown how adversity can be overcome. The more students can relate such stories to their own lives the more the stories will hold their attention and inspire.

Five inspirational stories

The following boxes present, in the words of the original tellers, four inspirational success stories. The first describes projects run by the charity Action for Sustainable Living in Manchester (Box 8.1). The second is an account of the Incredible Edible community project in Todmorden, on the edge of the Pennines (Box 8.2). The third is about street lighting in the Malvern Hills (Box 8.3), and the fourth describes an infant school and its commitment to the principles of sustainability (Box 8.4). They are a prompt to finding further examples of such stories to match the interests and needs of your own pupils or students.

Box 8.1 – Manchester: Action for Sustainable Living

As the name suggests, Action for Sustainable Living (AfSL) aims to support people in living more sustainably. In particular this is in the context of the individual's local community, so that local issues and priorities are tackled and resolved locally ... Action for Sustainable Living focuses on recruiting, training and supporting local people to promote sustainable living in all its various aspects. Action for Sustainable Living is a registered charity and a company limited by guarantee and has won many national awards.

CV Skills Growing

The project helps those who live in the Rusholme area and are unemployed gain skills for their CV whilst creating a community garden and growing their own fruit and veg. It also builds a link between the local Jobcentre Plus and its surrounding community.

A lack of volunteer opportunities for Jobcentre Plus customers in the Rusholme area means it is hard sometimes for those currently claiming out of work benefits to enhance their skills in a meaningful way. But Becky Kelly, a Jobcentre Plus adviser, was determined to investigate other ways of helping unemployed people in Rusholme boost their CVs. So, with the help and enthusiasm of her Action for Sustainable Living coordinator, Kate Wells, and building on her Local Project Management Training, Becky proposed a CV Skills Growing project, which would help those looking for work gain new skills, create a community garden and provide nutritious home-grown fruit and veg into the bargain. Currently five volunteers have signed up to take part in the project which is based at Trinity House Community Resource Centre. There have been numerous successful volunteer days (despite the weather!) and, with great enthusiasm, green spaces have been cleared and seeds and bulbs have been planted, ready for the growing season. The volunteers have also starred in a Jobcentre Plus promotional video short and featured on the Jobcentre Plus/Department for Work and Pensions intranet. 'It's really amazing to see the change in volunteers since the induction. They are all growing in confidence and seem to really be enjoying the project', said Becky.

RADISSON HOTEL ROOFTOP GARDEN

Paul Exall and Giles Bradley had been looking for a project to get their teeth into, ever since coming into contact with Action for Sustainable Living via the Local Project Manager's training. Coordinator Erika suggested they might be the right people for the job when the Radisson Hotel, wanting to engage more with the local community, started looking for a replacement gardener. Working with hotel staff and understanding the Radisson's longer term aims of operating in a more sustainable manner, Paul and Brad got cracking on enhancing their rooftop garden, helping to create a green oasis in the heart of the city centre where staff can relax, kitchen waste can be composted and nature can take its natural course.

Source: Action for Sustainable Living (2012)

BOX 8.2 – INCREDIBLE EDIBLE TODMORDEN

In the spring of 2008 ex-councillor Pam Warhurst and Mary Clear began planting vegetables all over their market town of Todmorden in West Yorkshire as part of Incredible Edible Todmorden (IET). It began with a patch of rhubarb beside a local bus stop and soon spread to graveyards, roundabouts and grassy patches by the side of the pavement. Then they published an advert in the local paper calling all of those 'interested in growing local food and sharing land' to attend a meeting. To their delight more than 60 people turned up and fantastic ideas were exchanged on how Todmorden's food supply could become self-sufficient. Since then, the whole town has come on board, including the local council, and the initiative is growing branches across the region.

FOOD SECURITY

Soon after Pam and Mary's community meeting, local residents began planting a community orchard, introducing polytunnels in local schools and sowing more vegetables in and around the town. The aim was to make Todmorden self-sufficient in vegetables, orchard fruits and eggs by 2018 and to rely mainly on local sources of meat. The project soon became a national talking point and public landowners saw that the benefits were reaching every corner of the town. Network Rail decided to donate more land for vegetable plots, the local council allocated land for a community orchard, and funding for 500 fruit trees and berry bushes has been granted.

COMMUNITY COHESION AND HEALTH

Almost every sector of the community got on board with the project, working together to make their town more self-sufficient. The local health people allowed IET to change the standard prickly planting with edibles, ornamental trees were replaced with fruit trees, and a medicinal herb garden was created. A local care home for the elderly allowed IET to create raised beds for community growing and permitted 'healing horticulture' – working with people with long-term mental health problems to grow there as part of their therapy. And Pennine Housing, the local registered social landlord, provided tenants with land to grow food and offered gardening packs, including plants, seeds and grow sacks to encourage tenants to grow their own. IET set up Every Egg Matters and created a map pinpointing poultry keepers who sell their surplus eggs when available. The group has grown from just four to over forty, and is still growing.

This widespread involvement in Incredible Edible Todmorden's food-growing activities has helped create a sense of community cohesion in Todmorden, which has had a positive impact, leading to a reduction in anti-social behaviour. A plot of derelict land behind the high school was offered by the council to be used for an orchard and beehives. This improved the look of the area, which added to a sense of community pride and ownership, and changed the way in which it was used by locals. The town has started to consider derelict and previously unsightly land as a resource and an asset, rather than as a liability.

EDUCATION

Incredible Edible Todmorden works with all the local schools to help get them growing food. The local church collaborated with children from the primary school to cultivate raised beds in the cemetery, and nearly all the schools in Todmorden have planted up a growing boat, using disused pleasure boats. One primary school has a small orchard and 26 raised beds for community use, and a local secondary school has invested in a commercial-size polytunnel and has integrated growing into the curriculum; they now have specialist status for agriculture and land-based industries.

In December 2009 local councillors helped Todmorden High School become more self-sufficient as the council's Cabinet committee agreed to a number of steps, which sought to help staff and students develop an aquaponics system. The Council dedicated the plot of land for the aquaponics system, and partnered with the Big Lottery to provide funding. Councillor Craig Whittaker, portfolio holder for Children and Young People's Services, said he was delighted the Council had been able to help the school progress with its proposals. He stated:

> Todmorden has led the way in creating a sustainable community and their efforts have already made national headlines. The school has been at the heart of the Incredible Edible project and this latest proposal demonstrates their commitment and passion for the scheme. This is a really

exciting project which will ultimately lead to the school being able to use the fish and vegetables they have cultivated in home economic lessons and the school canteen. Any surplus stock can then be sold on to the community... It will also allow the school to offer further education opportunities as students aged between 14 and 19 will be able to study for a BTEC diploma in Environment and Land Based Studies.

Source: Landshare (2011) at www.landshare.net/
case-studies/incredible-edible-todmorden/

Box 8.3 - Malvern Hills: The Gasketeers

Malvern is home to some of the UK's most beautiful gas lamps, said to have been C.S. Lewis's inspiration for the lamp in *The Lion, the Witch and the Wardrobe*. However, today the 104 lamps are poorly maintained, produce little light, and each costs the council £130 for gas and £450 for maintenance, but they are listed and central to the area's heritage.

Enter the Transition Malvern Hills Lighting Group, known as the 'Gasketeers', who, bringing together local and international expertise, have developed ways to refurbish the lamps (using local subcontractors) – improving their light output and preserving their unique character while significantly reducing their gas consumption, maintenance cost and light pollution. Installing timer controls, new electronic ignitions, more efficient burners and reflectors has reduced gas use by an average of 84 per cent, and maintenance requirements to just one visit per year, the lamps now costing just £20 for gas and £50 for maintenance per year. They are ten times brighter than before, and create no light pollution at all. They will also last 100 years, compared with the 30 years for conventional sodium lamps. The Gasketeers have even begun exploring how the lamps could be run on biomethane, improving on the carbon footprint of electric streetlights.

They calculated that if they were a professional consultancy, their work would be valued above £20,000, but they offered it free to the councils and community. They found that the most effective way to achieve success with such projects was to research and demonstrate feasibility, and obtain the support of the town and parish councils. All repairs are done by Lynn Jones, the UK's first female gas lamp technician, who does her maintenance rounds with everything she needs (including her ladder) on a bicycle trailer. C.S. Lewis would have approved, I imagine.

Source: Hopkins (2011: 147)

BOX 8.4 – SOUTH FARNBOROUGH INFANT SCHOOL

South Farnborough Infant School used what it learnt on the Ashden 'LESS CO_2' course to change its attitude towards energy use and help the next generation see the importance of treating energy responsibly. Substantial electricity and gas savings have been made despite the limitations of the building, thanks to a clear policy of monitoring, setting targets, energy management, technical changes and education.

A culture of sustainability and responsibility is at the core of this school with a clear understanding at all levels of the need to monitor and reduce energy consumption. Governors and the Head Teacher have agreed policies that are implemented by both paid and voluntary staff as well as pupils. The policies also extend to contractors working within the school. The school now pays for a Teacher in Charge of Sustainability to coordinate curriculum activities, oversee energy monitoring and ensure agreed targets are achieved.

In 2009–10 a teacher at the school attended the pilot 'LESS CO_2'. This coincided with the installation of a condensing boiler at the school. These two factors led the school to reflect on its energy use for the first time, and to start making changes. The first step was to start reading electricity and gas meters regularly. At first this was done monthly by the caretaker, and now daily by pupils. A smart meter now allows electricity usage data to be stored and compared month on month and through holiday periods. A daily target for electricity has been set and pupils monitor this via a display in the school hall with results being read out to the whole school at weekly assemblies. Pupils in the Green Gang monitor the switching off of electrical equipment within the school and award green tokens for good practice and red ones for non-compliance. Overall electricity consumption by the whole school has dropped by about 17% in the last year, saving around £1000 annually. 2010 saw the installation of a new gas boiler and measures to save energy on heating being introduced, with the result that gas consumption is down 24%, saving £5000 a year. As a result of the reductions in energy usage the school has reduced CO_2 emissions by about 36 tonnes per year.

'Care of our World' is promoted across the school curriculum both in school and out to the wider community. In early Years 'Eddie the Penguin' helps very young children understand the effects climate change is having and the simple things they can do to contribute to sustainable living. In Year One pupils learn about transport and its effects then move on to 'Houses and Homes' culminating in the design of shoe box 'Eco Houses' incorporating low energy features. They each make promises to reduce their impact on the environment and study the school environment, mini-beasts and wild flowers. All pupils take home an energy monitor to extend their studies by measuring electricity consumption at home.

Every family is asked to take part in the Two Week Energy Challenge. They borrow an electricity monitor from the school and log their daily electrical consumption, living as normal for the first week and making an effort to save electricity in the second. At the end of the challenge readings are brought back to the school and the prize of an energy monitor given to the household that has saved the most electricity. Following this activity one household reduced their electricity consumption by 44%.

The success of South Farnborough lies in achieving significant energy reductions without high capital cost or the use of expensive technology. By making staff and pupils aware of costs, empowering them to make changes and supporting them when necessary real cost benefits and energy savings have been made. This is a model that can be repeated in virtually every school and college and is particularly relevant at this time of economic restraint.

Source: Extracts from www.ashden.org/
winners/farnborough13

The Transition Network uses stories in a variety of ways These are not the same as actual success stories but are 'stories from/of a successful future.' *The Transition Companion* (Hopkins, 2011) contains stories from a 'powered-down future', focusing in particular on food, building and energy. Box 8.5 provides a flavour from those stories of what life could be like in 2030.

BOX 8.5 – STORIES FROM THE FUTURE

FOOD

By 2030, the system that feeds us looks very different. There has been a food and farming revolution across the UK. The oil price volatility that began in 2011 focused the nation's minds; rebuilding the nation's food security became urgent. Just as in the early days of the Second World War, there was a national crash-training in intensive food gardening, with free courses across the country. Most colleges and schools made food growing a central part of the curriculum, and lots of self-organised groups trained and supported each other in learning how to grow food, sharing tools and saving seeds. Food hubs popped up all over the country, which helped small-scale growers sell directly to the consumer, cutting out the middle man and helping to make small-scale growing viable ... .

BUILDINGS

By 2011 there was a strong move towards greener building and zero-carbon housing. However, much of what was built was falling short of the targets set by government. Construction that did reach better performance levels, although producing buildings that used little energy once built, relied heavily on very energy-intensive materials. It was commonplace for the bulk of materials to be imported long distances, and it was at about this time that the concept of 'building miles', akin to 'food miles', started to be looked at seriously ... .

ENERGY

The third area of our lives that has been transformed over the 20 years to 2030 is our relationship with how our energy is generated. The first place where the difference is noticeable is regarding how much less energy is used today. Compared with 2011, the UK now uses 55 per cent less energy than it did; energy has been saved through the retrofitting and increased energy-efficiency of schools, homes, offices, public buildings and industrial premises, and increased transport

---

efficiency. Gone are the days of office lighting left blazing all night, shops pumping hot air into the street and energy-guzzling appliances. Expectations of thermal comfort are lower. In winter people rightly expect to be warm, but part of that warmth now comes from the jumpers they are wearing rather than from the gas they are burning.

(Hopkins, 2011: 54 – 66)

Ideas for teaching
1. Incredible Edible
Suggested questions are:

- What are the advantages of food being grown in and around the local community?
- Where and how can one find out more about Incredible Edible Todmorden and how it works? See for example the short video 'Todmorden's local food revolution' at: www.guardian.co.uk/lifeandstyle/video/2010/oct/19/incredible-edible-todmorden
- Where else have similar local food growing schemes sprung up around the country?
- Why do you think these initiatives have been described as 'a local food revolution?'
- What FAQs can the class come up with and how might one find answers to them?

2. South Farnborough Infants
Suggested questions:

- Which of the activities at South Farnborough Infants do you find the most interesting and why?
- Are there any schools near you which have done similar things?
- Do you think that your own school might be able to do something similar? What might be a good way to begin this process?
- What reasons can you come up with that would persuade the Head and Governors to consider this?
- Who in the local community might also be able to help the school begin this process?

3. Stories from the future

Stories of this kind are intended to inspire. They are 'imagined' success stories, in this case setting out what a post-carbon future might look like. They use futures thinking and envisioning to devise positive future scenarios of successful community transition. Preferred scenarios are stories in their own right – guiding stars or beacons that draw us forward. 'Yes, this is the direction we need to go in. This is what we need to do now if we are to reach that place.' The glimpses in this chapter from *The Transition Companion* (Hopkins, 2011) can be used to prompt various lines of classroom research or teacher input. Such as:

- Identify the key features of each of these three glimpses of a post-carbon future and why they are important.
- What examples can you find of food, buildings and energy initiatives, locally or nationally, that are trying to achieve similar post-carbon goals today?
- List the things that might need to happen between now and a post-carbon future to help this shift come about.
- In what order do you think the steps need to come? In collaboration with a partner write a short story that shows how an initiative you know of in the present became the preferred future shown in one of the three glimpses.

Current examples of actual success stories can be found in *Transition Free Press News* at www.transitionfreepress.org

4. Finding other stories

Having sampled and discussed various success stories, pupils could be set the task of finding examples of their own. This might be from books, online or be about people and places they know. A clear focus will facilitate the search and could usefully relate to one of the eight doorways to sustainability: food and drink, energy and water, travel and traffic, purchasing and waste, buildings and grounds, inclusion and participation, local well-being, and the global dimension. Children could discuss which is their favourite success story and why.

Five things a school can do

- Staff should read the first part of this chapter and further identify what they believe to be the elements of good success stories for children.
- Make an inventory of known success stories, and their focus and suitability for different age groups, and actively seek new examples.

- Staff development could include the sharing of newly found success stories and discussion on how best to use them.
- Some of these stories should be shared with the community and they could be read out by the children who first enjoyed them.
- A visit from a professional story-teller is always good value, especially if she/he tells stories appropriate to the post-carbon agenda.

Chapter 9

Visualizing the future

At the heart of this book is my concern that teachers and students think critically and creatively about the future. Chapter 5 explored some of the reasons why this might have been avoided so far but unless we clarify the future we would prefer it will be left to powerful groups in society, such as investment bankers and overpaid CEOs who fail to understand the limits to growth. This chapter looks at two important tools that can be used for thinking about the future: scenarios and envisioning.

The value of scenarios

Future scenarios are designed to provide a series of different pictures of the future so we can explore ways in which the future might work out. Employed by business, planners, service providers, futurists and others, scenarios are a tool for exploring the question 'What if…?' Traditionally, scenarios offer four or five different versions of a future that could arise from present conditions. The positives and negatives of each are considered, as well as the reasons each might come about, and what, therefore, might need to be done in the present to facilitate or block different scenarios.

'In futures studies,' writes Sam Cole, 'scenarios are ideally developed from a mix of verbal, empirical, theoretical, philosophical, and anecdotal information; fantasy, fact, and fiction. In general, a scenario consists of a selection of variables, their past trends and the interactions between them, and some assumptions about future changes. This information may be expressed in a combination of structured visual, verbal, and quantitative ways' (Cole, 2002: 243–4).

In other words scenarios are not just thought up on the spur of the moment but are the result of careful analysis of past, present and possible future trends. In their final form, future scenarios may be extremely detailed and come with relevant documentation to elaborate them. They are emphatically *not* predictions about the future, but rather a tool for discussing probable and preferable futures. I'm not a futurist *per se*, so I will highlight in summary form some scenarios suitable for use with older school students.

In educational terms scenarios tend to be brief and designed to offer tasters or glimpses of the future. They are intended to prompt discussion rather than offering a detailed picture. My first example (Box 9.1) is taken from a project called Climate Futures, a detailed study drawn up by Forum for the Future (2013), for business use, which 'analyses the social, political, economic and psychological consequences of climate change and describes how different global responses to the problem could lead to five very different worlds by 2030'.

BOX 9.1 – CLIMATE-FUTURE SCENARIOS

EFFICIENCY FIRST

Rapid innovation in energy efficiency technologies has created a consumerist, low carbon world. Yet society balances precariously on a fine point, with ever-increasing reliance on new innovations to mitigate continuing climate change. Massive desalination plants in the Middle East and North Africa soak up energy from the sun to irrigate the desert for resource production. Wilderness exists in only a few pockets of the world.

SERVICE TRANSFORMATION

High carbon prices have resulted in businesses rethinking their models and selling services rather than products. Individual car ownership is prohibitive but the public transport system is highly efficient. Collective laundry services have replaced washing machines. A 'share with your neighbour' ethos exists and global carbon emissions decline for the first year in history.

REDEFINING PROGRESS

People are rethinking what it means to lead a fulfilling life. Meaningful jobs are valued and stronger links with local communities are cultivated. People are attracted to simplicity and focus much more on quality of life than economic prosperity. Climate change is well understood and viewed as one part of unsustainable living.

ENVIRONMENTAL WAR ECONOMY

Governments have left it late to deal with climate change and have been forced to rationalize whole industry sectors and take control of many aspects of citizens' lives. They build dams and powerful sea wall defences to protect land from the raging oceans, yet growing numbers of environmental refugees must find new countries willing to accommodate them. Greenhouse gases are beginning to decline, but the cost to individual liberty has been great.

> PROTECTIONIST WORLD
> The world is divided into protectionist blocs, and countries wage violent wars over scarce resources like water. Communities are divided and cyber-terrorists take advantage of the flux, paralyzing communication networks and targeting collapsed states.
>
> *Source*: Forum for the Future (2013)

If one was using these scenarios with older pupils some of the questions arising would be:

- What must have happened between now and 2030 for each of these scenarios to have come about?
- What would be the advantages and disadvantages of living in each of these scenarios?
- What questions arise for you about people's differing responses to climate change?
- If not these scenarios, then what other alternatives might there be? Elaborate on your own preferred scenario and explain the factors that could lead to this coming about.

As these examples show, scenarios often have pithy titles that sum up their focus. One traditional set of scenarios, which takes a broader view of human futures, is: Business as Usual, Technological Fix, Edge of Disaster and Sustainable Development (Hicks, 2012a), summarized in Box 9.2.

> ## Box 9.2 – WORLD-FUTURE SCENARIOS
>
> ### BUSINESS AS USUAL
> This future has come about because people feel safe with things as they are and don't imagine things being very different. It is based on the assumption that things worked reasonably well in the past and will therefore continue to do so in the future. Similar problems will occur and be dealt with in similar ways to today. This future benefits those who are already well off and those who don't like change. It could, on the other hand, lead to an edge of disaster scenario.
>
> ### EDGE OF DISASTER
> This future has come about because people and governments responsible for making decisions were too slow to act. They worked on the assumption that the problems were not that serious. This

assumption was wrong and the scenario shows various disasters, not all of which would necessarily occur at the same time. However, for those living in the 'poor world', many of these disasters are already here as a result of 'rich world' policies. This future doesn't benefit anyone. It can, however, encourage people and governments to make significant changes in the way that they live.

TECHNOLOGICAL FIX

This future has come about because people felt that rapid growth of science and technology would solve all their problems. It is based on the assumption that what can be invented always should be invented. This future can bring many benefits but can also have many unforeseen consequences. At the same time it also involves dominating nature and thus cuts people off from the natural environment on which all life depends.

SUSTAINABLE DEVELOPMENT

This future has come about because people recognised the need for major change. It is based on the assumption that caring for the environment, other people and future generations also brings a better quality of life in the present. This future brings a less stressful and simpler lifestyle for many people. Developments in science and technology are used by the community to meet their own local needs.

Source: Hicks (2012a)

This set of scenarios was designed for classroom use with accompanying graphics. It needs to be made clear to students that such scenarios are not predictions about the future but rather possible futures that could occur in industrialized countries if different trends and events occurred. The questions for students that go with this set of visual scenarios are:

- Do you think people like living in this possible future?
- What are some of the good things about it?
- What are some of the difficult things about it?
- Who will benefit and who will lose in this future?
- Say why you would or wouldn't like to live in this future

More pertinent to the concerns of this book are the eight visual scenarios on aspects of a sustainable future that can be found in *Sustainable Schools, Sustainable Futures* (Hicks, 2012a). These are on food and farming, energy and water, travel and transport, consuming and wasting, buildings and biodiversity, inclusion and participation, and local well-being and global connections. An example can be found in Chapter 6 of this book.

The use of scenarios, therefore, is particularly to prompt discussion about differing alternative futures by illustrating a range of options. They could illustrate possible, probable or preferable futures, or often a mix of them. They are intended to provoke and puzzle. How could this future ever come about? Who could possibly want to live in this particular scenario? Who benefits and loses in each of the scenarios. Although many scenarios may appear in quite detailed form, they often also have a one-paragraph version (as here) to prompt the learner's immediate response. Further appropriate detail can be imagined as debate progresses.

Envisioning the future

Envisioning is another tool for exploring preferred futures. James Dator, director of the Hawaii Research Centre for Futures Studies, highlights the importance of this process when he writes:

> Futures studies tries to help people in becoming more active in envisioning a preferred future. To teach them to find the way they would want the future to be, and to act in their personal lives, business, or governments in order to achieve a better future. So, part of the activity we do in futures studies is helping people in envisioning a more plausible future than they might otherwise. And we do it by giving them a greater range of images, by helping them to choose the way they want the future to be so they can move in the right direction.
>
> (Dator, 2006)

How can we ever attain a goal that we cannot imagine? How can we ever attain a more sustainable future unless we have practised the skills of envisioning alternative futures? This is the first step in being able to identify where we want to get to, but not the only step. As Dennis Meadows writes:

> Visioning means imagining, at first generally and then with increasing specificity, what you really want. That is, *what you really want*, not what someone has taught you to want, and not what you have been willing to settle for. Visioning means taking off the constraints of 'feasibility', of disbelief and past disappointments, and letting your mind dwell upon its most noble, uplifting, treasured dreams ... We should say immediately, for the sake of sceptics, that we do not believe vision makes anything

happen. Vision without action is useless. But action without vision is directionless and feeble. Vision is absolutely necessary to guide and motivate. More than that, vision, when widely shared and firmly kept in sight, does *bring into being new systems.*

(Meadows *et al.* 2005: 272)

The process of envisioning can be carried out in various ways and requires a procedure that engages the affect and the imagination as much as the intellect. It cannot be adequately done over a cup of coffee but requires a quiet space in which the imagination can be focused. Envisioning workshops might be used by a community group to consider how they want their neighbourhood to change, by children considering how the school playground might be redeveloped, or by teenagers reflecting on their local needs before a meeting with local councillors. Envisioning is about identifying preferable futures, the ones we would most hope to see realized as a result of our deeply held values and our notion of the good life. The process requires a contemplative space where one can draw on images that initially come more from intuition and the heart than intellect and the head. In a contemplative space, images can arise from the subconscious that may surprise the conscious mind yet have the ring of truth about them.

Important early work on imaging or envisioning was carried out in the 1980s by Elise Boulding (1994) when she was working with peace activists who were concerned about the nuclear arms race. What she discovered was that while they were clear about what they opposed they often found it difficult to visualize the alternative they wished to see – a world without nuclear weapons. What would such a world look like? What would be the steps required to bring such a world about? She was not the first person to use envisioning workshops, but she was one of the first to help activists focus on what a nuclear-free world might actually look like. As her focus broadened, she began to work with all sorts of groups, ranging from church and community groups to businesses and other institutions.

Each group brought its own issues to the workshop, whereas Elise brought a process that would help each group to clarify the nature of their preferred future. Then the real work began: identifying the skills and strategies needed to help create their preferred future. In one sense this was easiest when the focus was on, say, a particular church, business or community; but for others the brief was much wider – the nature of a good society.

Boulding is one of the few people to have detailed the outcomes of such envisioning workshops and to have analysed the futures imagery that arises. In particular she notes the presence of several common themes she found.

> Whatever people are doing, women and men are doing it together. Children and the elderly seem to be everywhere – there is no age segregation. Communities are also described as racially mixed. Learning seems to take place 'on the job' ... This is a non-hierarchical world; no one is 'in charge'. It is also one in which locality is very important ... Technology is low profile, but it does exist and everyone reports that it is shared ... Although the new-consciousness theme varies in importance, there is widespread reporting that people are operating out of a different sense of awareness than that of the present.
>
> (Boulding, 1994: 73–4)

She describes a 'baseline future' common to most imaging groups that she has worked with. She reports a sense of 'boundarylessness' (a greater flow of people and ideas unimpeded by formal structures) and the use of the adjectives 'bright', 'clean' and 'green' to describe this preferred future world. She suggests that the recurrence of such images, regardless of the participant's background, might indicate some 'deep structures at work in the futures-imaging process that should be more fully explored' (ibid.: 82).

All envisioning workshops, or futures workshops as they are sometimes called, need to begin with an assessment of the present situation and the problems and dilemmas that need transforming, whether they concern professional life, a community issue or the need to clarify what a zero-carbon future might actually look like. In work with students I've sometimes used one of the eight doorways to sustainability as a focus, such as food and farming, energy or transport. If discussion has been more generally about the state of the world, I ask participants to hold in mind just one key aspect of their preferred future. What follows is essentially a guided journey in the imagination, best done with eyes closed and guided prompts from the teacher. Participants are asked to let images arise in response to questions such as 'What do you see around you in your preferred future?', 'What is different?', 'What has changed?' Note that the facilitator's task is solely to prompt the participant's imagination, not to suggest any images. Most people are surprised at how easily images arise in the mind's eye, although some adults report that they sense ideas rather than seeing actual images.

At the time I was running envisioning workshops I didn't focus on sustainability *per se* but rather on participants' preferred futures more widely. I drew on the work of various researchers who had developed procedures for envisioning preferred futures. Generally the envisioning process was part of a half-day workshop and the time horizon given as 25 years into the future. The first group were undergraduates studying Education, or students studying for a Post Graduate Certificate in Education (PGCE); the second were educators with an interest in social and global issues. After the visualization, participants worked individually and then in small groups, to flesh out the key features of their preferred future for society and made a poster to summarize it.

Box 9.3 is a summary of the key features of society that came up in the student groups and of the images that had arisen for them.

BOX 9.3 - STUDENTS' PREFERRED FUTURES: KEY FEATURES

Green – clean air and water, trees, wildlife, flowers

Convivial – cooperative, relaxed, happy, caring, laughter

Transport – no cars, no pollution, public transport, bikes

Peaceful – absence of violent conflict, security, global harmony

Equity – no poverty, fair shares for all, no hunger

Justice – equal rights of people and planet, no discrimination

Community – local, small, friendly, simpler, sense of community

Education – for all, on-going for life, holistic, community

Energy – lower consumption, renewable and clean sources

Work – for all, satisfying, shared, shorter hours

Healthy – better health care, alternative, longer life

Food – organic farming, locally grown, balanced diet

Source: Hicks (2006c)

These features are ranked in order of importance, and together offer an outline map of the preferred futures for these students. The students came from three different universities but were all studying education in one form or another. Most were in their late teens or early twenties. What strikes me is their interest in a more green, just and peaceful future. Although I didn't talk about sustainable futures at the time, this is exactly what they described. They were not asked to envision a sustainable future, but this is where their dreams led them. One of the PGCE students came up to me afterwards and said: 'Do you know, nobody has ever asked me before in my life what sort of society I would like to live in.' I could but answer: 'I think that is an educational crime!'

And what of educators themselves? In a longer residential workshop for social educators we explored the nature of their preferred futures and attempted to capture the essence of these in words and pictures. Box 9.4 highlights the main themes that emerged and the key features of their preferred futures.

Box 9.4 – Social educators' preferred futures: key features

Conviviality

Calmer pace of life – less stress – smiling, energetic people – time to talk – more joy but also sadness – richer quality of relationships – no rush, people relaxing – lots of laughter – comfortable and colourful clothes

Community

Locally produced goods – more jobs based at home – doors open, no burglar alarms – recycling schemes – groups open and welcoming to others – bartering and skills exchange – ease between the generations – digitally interactive notice boards for voting on local issues – unhurried and more reflective people – music and street theatre – deschooling

Towns

Human scale – clean and healthy – trees, gardens, fountains – energy efficient buildings – renewable energy – no supermarkets – small shops and market stalls – vibrant cultural centre – multicultural – people and children in spacious streets – sculptures, frescoes and public spaces – absence of mechanical noise – bustle of activity – no beggars or homeless – no cars – bike routes, trams and trains – organic gardening – easy access to countryside

Environment

A green manifesto – sunshine – birdsong, clean air, calm and beautiful countryside – forests, valleys, hills and lakes – flowers and animals – brightness and light – closer relationship with and greater respect for nature

Source: Hicks (2006d)

What strikes me is that with both the students and the social educators, the process tapped into the deepest aspects of what it means to be human – the need for safety, community, good relations, justice, a good environment– rather than being 'merely' the imagination, as one colleague argued. These findings also show, significantly, that without being asked or prompted, participants' preferred futures were also more sustainable futures. Identifying one's vision, as Meadows *et al.* argue (2005), uplifts, focuses and empowers the group for the next vital stage of committed planning and action. A comment I once overheard at someone else's envisioning workshop was: 'Well, that was a total waste of time, I could have done it over a cup of coffee.' This is to totally misunderstand the purpose of the process; there is a major difference between pondering something over a drink or meditating over it until tapping deep insights.

Lessons for the future

1. Using scenarios

The sets of scenarios discussed at the start of this chapter, on Climate Futures and World Futures, are each accompanied by questions intended to provoke discussion and debate. The scenarios, though intentionally brief, are sufficient to prompt critical and creative reflection on how they might have come about, on which seem most probable and on which feel most preferable.

Using scenarios in this way should be set in a wider context, in this case climate change or global issues. The future is still to be decided by our considered, or unconsidered, actions in the present. Scenarios work best for young people if they have a visual component, as in the example in Chapter 6 (Figure 6.1). It is taken from a set of eight visual scenarios depicting aspects of a more sustainable future, a free download available from Worldwide Fund for Nature (Hicks, 2012a). Teachers and pupils could create their own visual scenarios to relate to specific local and global issues.

2. A procedure for envisioning

The procedure I've used for envisioning preferred futures was developed over a number of years from different sources, although I've worked mainly with teachers and trainee teachers rather than with children. There are also three important provisos to be made. First, there is little value in running an envisioning session as a one-off because, lacking a context for what they are doing, participants tend not to take it seriously. It is best, therefore, if it is part of a course or one of several sessions on global issues, futures, climate change, sustainability or whatever, i.e. areas that require a futures-orientated element. Second, participants sometimes jib at being asked to close their eyes, but I suggest it helps to focus the imagination. I once overheard a teacher say to her colleague, 'Wasn't that embarrassing, it felt like prayers in assembly.' I suspect that what sometimes happens is that closing one's eyes in the company of others makes one feel vulnerable. Third, it is important to stress that the process is about tapping the active imagination rather than the intellect. It is about letting images arise from the subconscious in response to prompts from the facilitator, a sort of semi-guided meditation. Here is the sequence of steps I used:

1. *Settling down* – Tell the group they are going to experience a process that can help them explore what their preferred post-carbon future might look like. This does not involve sitting down and thinking about it, but rather it allows images to arise from the subconscious, where a rich store of imagery is to be found. Ask the participants to relax and make themselves comfortable and then to close their eyes – which my students were always reluctant to do at first.

2. *Warming up* – The next step is to 'warm up' the imagination as it were. Ask the group to recall a special or favourite place in their mind's eye and ask them to look at the detail. 'What time of day is it? What are the colours you can see? What can you smell? What are the sounds, the textures?' Give the group enough time to be really present to their chosen place. Affirm that some might have clear images, others less so, and that some may sense their favourite place in other ways.

3. *Beginning the journey* – Remind the group that they are going on a journey to glimpse some elements of their preferred post-carbon future. Ask them to see themselves in their imagination exiting the building but finding the scene outside changed. In front of them, stretching to left and right as far as the eye can see, is a tall hedge they can't see over. Their preferred future lies on the other side. Ask them to look at the colour and texture of the hedge. Then draw their attention to a gateway in the hedge. 'What does it look like? What is it made of?' Always leave a space between prompts for the participants to engage in the process.

4. *Entering the future* – Ask the participants to look closely at the details of the gate. 'How does it open? Does it open easily?' And then after passing through the archway, 'Where are you? ... Do you find yourself inside or outside? ... Is it somewhere you recognize? ... Wherever you find yourself just trust the images that arise ... Look around you, what can you see? ... What are the colours, textures, sounds and smells of this future? ... How is it different from today? ... What are people doing that is different? ...

What are people saying that is different?' This stage should take 5–10 minutes depending on how you feel the group is responding.

5. *Gifts of the future* – Continue: 'It will soon be time to return to your present. Look around you and note the most important elements of this future that you wish to remember. What are they? ... It is now time to leave and you need to make your farewells ... Is there anything you need to say or do before you leave? ... Now it's time to turn and walk back to the hedge ... What does it look like from this side? ... As you return through the gateway you return to the present. You enter the building and find yourself back in this room ... Do not open your eyes yet. Just sit quietly and note the things you have brought back from this journey. When you are ready, but without talking to anybody, jot down what you need to remember.'

6. *Working together* – Each participant then finds a partner to work with and in turn share their experience. No questions should be asked until both have done so. Then ask some clarifying questions. 'Can you tell me a bit more about that? Can you describe that a bit more? Why do you think that felt important to you?' Then each pair draws a composite poster illustrating the key features of their futures. 'What are the similarities? What are the differences?' The poster needs to be as self-explanatory as possible.

7. *Debriefing* – The posters are displayed around the room. When everyone has seen them all, ask them for their first impressions of the post-carbon futures before them. Are there any common themes? Ask whether they have any questions about particular posters, stressing that there are no 'right' answers. Whatever came to people during the activity is right for them. Conclude by inviting discussion about what has been learnt from these preferable futures and how they felt about the process itself.

Five things a school can do

- Staff should be introduced to the notion of scenarios and work together to produce post-carbon scenarios for the school.
- Staff can reflect on the local community and come up with possible post-carbon scenarios for the local area.
- Discuss what needs to be done to help bring the preferred post-carbon scenario about.

- Find volunteers to take part in an envisioning activity. Try it out and modify it for greatest effectiveness. You could use this process to explore the preferred scenarios in greater detail.
- Use these and other techniques suggested in this book to build up a detailed picture of a post-carbon school and community.

Part Four

Education for transition

4

The Wales Institute for Sustainable Education
Centre for Alternative Technology at Machynlleth

Chapter 10

Post-carbon scenarios

Where have we got to?

So what are the options facing us? The starkest are those relating to any system in ecological overshoot – collapse or managed decline. We may like to argue that human civilization is different from other ecosystems, but the indicators are that there are only two ways out. Yes, there is a voice in my head which says 'No, we're different. And anyway this is too big for me to even try and comprehend!' But it's prudent to accept that these really *are* the only two choices we have. I am reminded of the words in Shakespeare's *King Lear* – 'Ripeness is all'. When fruit is ripe only two outcomes are possible. It can fall to the ground and rot (collapse) or alternatively it can be consumed and transformed (managed decline) in the service of life. Managed decline may take much longer than we think, as David Orr asserts: 'The multiple problems of climate change and sustainability will not be solved by this generation, or even the next. Our challenge is to get the name of the thing right and do so in such a way as to create the possibility that they might someday be resolved' (Orr, 2009: 92).

I have variously used the adjectives low carbon, zero carbon and post-carbon in this book, while others may talk of transition or sustainable futures. We may not have got the name right yet, but we have the beginnings of a new lexicon that only later commentators will resolve.

Chapter 5 introduced the notion of scenarios as a useful tool for exploring future options, and it is useful here in reflecting on different possible post-carbon futures. As we saw, scenarios are not predictions about the future but rather possible alternative futures. It is up to the user to decide which, if any, are probable or preferable. In arriving at the four scenarios used in this chapter I have been influenced by other authorities referred to in this book, in particular Holmgren and Elliott and Urry. In these scenarios I have kept close to a standard pattern, choosing four to illustrate what would happen if (a) nothing were done at all; (b) technology were to win the day, (c) things were to go really badly, or (d) the best possible outcome were to be achieved. They are intended to prompt discussion about what our priorities should be for the future in the face of the hazards that lie ahead. All four scenarios are couched in general terms and can be rewritten to illustrate a particular country, region, town or community. The reader might come up with a quite different set of scenarios. 'Amend and improve' are the watchwords of the coming transition.

The four scenarios

Each scenario is set out first in short summary form in Box 10.1. The initial task with any set of scenarios is to see what discussion they prompt. This is best done in pairs or small groups and then fed into larger group discussion. How does each scenario affect you? What thoughts do you have? What feelings? Which seems the most probable? Which feels the most preferable? What other scenarios would you want to suggest? Remember that scenarios are not designed to give you answers but to help clarify future options and choices; and of course they oversimplify.

BOX 10.1 – FOUR POST-CARBON SCENARIOS

How might society change as a result of climate change, peak oil and the limits to growth, over the next forty years or so? This will depend on how governments, business, communities and individuals interact in the face of such challenges. Here are four outline scenarios of different possible futures.

BUSINESS AS USUAL

This future came about because governments and businesses felt that continued economic growth was the safest way forward. It had been tried and tested in the past and it was felt best to stay with what was already known. In terms of energy use the emphasis continued to be on fossil fuels – oil, coal and gas, with some renewable sources. On account of public complaints about wind power, this energy sector remained small. It was also felt that the effects of climate change were being over-exaggerated and funding that could have gone into mitigation and adaptation went instead into new nuclear power stations. The notion of there being limits to growth was seen as a problem that new technology would resolve. As a result of these decisions, significant climate change occurred, for which both people and government were ill-prepared and society suffered accordingly.

TECHNO-STABILITY

This future came about because the UK government took a central role in encouraging society to move away from the use of fossil fuels and towards a post-carbon society based on extensive use of renewable

---

149

energy sources. This led to a steep drop in carbon emissions, which encouraged other countries, somewhat belatedly, to follow suit. This was also matched by an expansion of green technologies in every aspect of daily life, which played a significant part in mitigating climate change and also in helping people adapt to the ongoing changes caused by it. This stress on green technologies was not only about energy production, but also about transport, communications, building and agriculture. It helped to reduce the impact of new growth and expansion on the environment and led to an overall decrease in the size of the country's ecological footprint.

ENERGY CRASH

This future came about because the government failed to give a clear lead in the transition to a low-carbon future, trying to continue business as usual to keep people happy and failing to invest sufficiently in renewable energy sources. As fossil fuel prices went up and global warming increased, people felt uncertain about the best way forward. Electricity blackouts became more frequent and only those people who had invested in renewable energies on their own initiative could guarantee staying warm and keeping the lights on. In this muddled energy descent little investment went into mitigation or adaptation, so that climate change became an increasing hazard. While lip service was paid to the idea that there were limits to growth, it turned out to be no more than words. Since there was no consensus on what should be done, people found they were often left to fend for themselves in their own communities.

SUSTAINABLE TRANSITION

This future came about because people, businesses and government saw the benefits of a more decentralized and resilient society in coping with the changes that were occurring. As ideas on sustainability began to spread, it became clear that fossil fuels had to be phased out as soon as possible and renewable energy sources brought in. Communities tackled this in different ways, but it worked because people felt a real responsibility for their own suburb, town and region. This went hand in hand with mitigation and adaptation projects to limit the effects of climate change and to make local communities more resilient. Since the limits to growth were also recognized at the community level, it became easier for changes to be made at the grassroots. More elements of a sustainable future thus came into existence and the greater self-reliance of communities made climate change somewhat more easy to bear.

Source: Author

A somewhat expanded version of each scenario now follows, to put more flesh on the bones.

The scenarios in more detail

1. Business as usual

In this scenario it was generally thought that climate change would not be as bad as some predicted and that it could be dealt with in a piecemeal fashion. This meant that action to mitigate its impact and to adapt to changing conditions was weak. In the absence of any clear direction, public responses ranged from the confused to the chaotic. The notion of peak oil was generally dismissed and fossil fuels continued to play a major role in meeting energy demand. Although various renewable energy initiatives went ahead, global warming still increased for later generations. Fuel prices became more volatile, and hiccups began to occur in the energy supply chain.

The notion of there being limits to growth was marginalized and seen as an issue that could be resolved through materials substitution and technological improvement. Most people therefore welcomed the opportunity to continue spending and consuming, although some, by choice or through economic necessity, did not. The consequence of this scenario was that ecological overshoot came earlier each year. Yet the public were generally resistant to the notion of transition and could not comprehend the possibility that industrial society contained within itself the seeds of its own demise. While a growing minority tried to challenge this consensus there was general confusion over what one was expected to do or not to do. Communities therefore found themselves increasingly divided and in disarray over these matters.

The industrial model of agriculture began to falter, food supplies were kept up at first but periodic shortages became more common. There was a small but growing organic sector, which arose in the face of these difficulties of supply. Underlying the dilemmas related to food and farming was, in essence, a clash of paradigms about how agriculture worked best. For most people, however, the issues were price rises and intermittent empty shelves. At home and at work it gradually became clear that the existing building stock was inadequate in the face of extreme weather, rain, floods and drought. While there was token retrofitting of old building stock and scattered examples of new 'green build', no clear guidance was given on what should be done.

Travel and transport continued much as before at first, although price and availability of fuel became more erratic. In particular, life became more difficult for motorists, although new hybrid vehicles were coming in and the range of electric-powered vehicles increased. Traffic jams and long delays became more common in towns and on motorway routes. Cutbacks and the privatization of the health service continued despite the occurrence of new diseases and a return of some once thought to have been eliminated. What became known as 'climate change depression' increased, and some people began to turn more towards alternative medicine and health care.

While the government encouraged the populace to 'stay calm and carry on', this was increasingly seen as an inadequate response to the multiple challenges. Widespread online discussion and debate demonstrated increasing levels of dissatisfaction across the country but produced no clear agreement on what was wrong or what should be done. Postal and web services were sometimes down, as were radio and TV broadcasts. Changes became more evident in biodiversity as temperatures and weather patterns changed. New diseases attacked flora and fauna with increasingly significant loss of species. At the same time, new species of insects and pests presented as yet unknown threats to farming and health.

'Business as usual' thus led to a period of deep uncertainty and insecurity, increasingly steep economic decline and the fragmentation of society. With no clear guidance on the key issues, unsustainable practices became more common at local, regional and national levels. Sustainability itself became a distant dream for those who had hoped for a better future – a future that might once have been but was no longer possible.

2. Techno-stability

In this scenario it was understood that both climate change and peak oil represented serious threats to society – ones that needed to be countered with all possible resources. It was taken for granted that human ingenuity and technological expertise could overcome any dilemma, whatever the scale of the problem. For example, techno-mitigation in relation to global warming prioritized carbon capture and storage, so that CO_2 emissions from coal-fired power stations were greatly reduced. Techno-adaptation involved wide-scale use of the latest developments in green engineering and technology, applied to building construction, to the growing of food and to methods of transport. This was only possible because of the centralized response to the crisis. There was some reduction in the use of fossil fuel, with more renewable sources being brought online, together with the construction of new-design nuclear power stations. Strict legislation on energy conservation was also introduced in relation to both domestic and work usage.

While the notion of there being limits to growth was generally recognized, it was not felt to be an immediate issue since hi-tech responses were seen as the first line of defence against climate change and peak oil. Limits were set on consumerist expectations of 'business as usual', so trimming public expectations to meet the new challenges ahead. The stress on techno-fix solutions was seen as appropriate and natural by younger people, although some older members of the community felt this route was also being used to cover up deeper underlying issues. Better and quicker networking became available between and within communities, although some unevenness was still present across the country as a whole.

One of the main breakthroughs was in the field of genetically modified (GM) crops, where resistance from environmental groups was overridden by new pro-GM legislation. This was felt to be hugely important, because the industrial model of agriculture increasingly faced higher prices for oil-based fuel, fertilizers and pesticides. A small organic sector flourished in response to concern about the hi-tech developments in farming and food production. At the same time a significant retrofitting programme began to improve energy use in old housing stock together with increased new builds based on sustainable principles.

The face of transport also began to change. Public transport by road, rail and even canal improved so cars were used less. Hybrid and electric vehicles became cheaper so more common. One school of thought held that travelling less should become the norm, given the possibility of virtual travel and online meetings. With the appearance of new health hazards arising from global warming, emphasis was placed on better, more modern healthcare. Drugs and medicines became more easily available to meet changing conditions. In this high-tech society electronic communications were generally good, as were most other communication systems. However, occasional blackouts still occurred as the result of glitches in the development of new systems, a reminder that while human ingenuity may seem limitless its application can never be perfect.

'Techno-stability' offered a positive way ahead in the face of major global changes, but it was only possible through governmental diktat and the pouring of existing resources (human, financial and technological) into green tech solutions. This was sustainability bought at the price of limits to growth, a provisional utopia that might not necessarily last.

3. Energy crash

In this scenario climate change proved to be worse than expected, its impact coming sooner than anticipated and its consequences more severe. Only limited attempts were made at mitigation and little was done in the way of adaptation, whether in relation to energy conservation, extreme weather, flooding or drought. Most people were therefore totally unprepared for what was to come. It was a case of too little, too late. Some small reduction was made in the use of fossil fuels and some initial advances made in relation to solar and wind energy, but there was little real understanding of the need for a major shift towards renewable sources of energy. Peak oil made energy supplies increasingly expensive and they began to falter as the national grid failed to keep up with demand. Increasingly people were at the mercy of the elements.

Despite accelerated climate change, the limits to growth debate was not prioritized, although major resource shortages and fast rising prices for everyday goods inevitably reduced patterns of consumption. The virtue of 'make do and mend' thus returned to social and economic life. Under these pressures communities became more fragmented and vulnerable. Life became much tougher than people were used to, and it was the powerful in society and the hoarders of resources that survived best. Attempts were made to achieve greater levels of local resilience, but these were limited by the struggle for day-to-day survival.

Global food supplies began to falter as the system came under increasing pressure, resulting in long queues and empty shelves in the shops. Levels of nourishment declined and ill health increased. Frequent hoarding began. Best-off were those who could grow most of their own food. Buildings were generally inadequate to the rigours of climate change, but energy supplies became increasingly erratic, witnessing widespread blackouts. Communities were left to muddle through as best they could, with little guidance or support.

Transport systems began to break down and long distance travel was increasingly difficult. People had to resort to older forms of transport: foot, cycle, boat, horse and cart. Travel became much more localized and took place only when really necessary. The health system began to break down as people's health deteriorated and disease increased. Heath support was limited and also more localized, as people resorted to older and simple remedies, where they were known.

Eventually most systems of communication went down and only occasional emergency broadcasts were made. News from outside the local area became extremely limited and was only available on a face-to-face basis and was seldom reliable. Biodiversity was increasingly damaged as natural resources became subject to hunting and scavenging. Under these conditions there was little sense of social or environmental responsibility.

Total unpreparedness for the impact of climate change, peak oil and the limits to growth led not just to the decline of society but to its almost total collapse. Born to believe that 'progress' was part of one's birthright, industrial societies disappeared just as surely as earlier empires had. This scenario occurred because of the twentieth-century conceit that we, unlike our ancestors, were invincible because we could conquer all with our ingenuity and technological skills and overcome all difficulties – except our own demise.

4. Sustainable transition

In this scenario climate change was taken seriously at both national and local levels and concerted action was taken in pursuit of both mitigation and adaptation. The dilemma of peak oil was widely recognized nationally and locally and the need for a shift towards a post-carbon society recognized. Decentralized forms of renewable energy generation were encouraged and major off-shore wind arrays and solar collectors created. Encouragement for this major shift came from local, regional and national government, backed by extensive programmes of work in schools, further and higher education.

The limits to growth were also taken seriously and national targets were set for the reversal of ecological overshoot day. This resulted in a new public understanding of the hazards of excess consumerism and the need for communities and the country as a whole to become more self-reliant and resilient. This led to a much deeper understanding of sustainability and unsustainability, spearheaded by innovative work in schools with those who would become responsible for their communities and society in the future. Local authorities and parish councils increasingly joined forces with transition initiatives to realize the goals of a more sustainable society.

An increasing emphasis on food security led to the reorganization of agriculture to meet national needs, so that food shortages were generally avoided. The new post-carbon approach to farming, necessitated by increasingly high costs of fertilizers and herbicides, meant a shift away from the world of agribusiness and towards organic growing. People became used to eating more local and seasonal food and public health improved. Many more people grew some of their own food, whether in gardens, allotments or as part of community schemes. It was also a time of massive change in relation to building and house design. A national programme of retrofitting all older properties to meet zero carbon standards created a significant number of new jobs. A new interest in traditional methods of building soon grew and all new build properties were designed to meet the highest eco-standards. Much of this work was community focused, generating wide interest and debate.

All long journeys were now by fast and efficient public transport. The trains and coaches were interconnected with local transport systems involving electric vehicles, trams, cycle ways, walkways and canals. Generally people travelled less than before, enjoying the benefits of their own community and region. These changes led to a fitter and healthier population. There was a more efficient mainstream health service that dovetailed with alternative and complementary approaches to health care.

Although digital forms of communication remained important, there was a shift to greater face-to-face communication, with practical skills often being learnt on an intergenerational and community basis. Life became a more directly participatory venture, with an emphasis on supportive communication skills and conflict resolution skills. The need to protect the changing face of local and national biodiversity was widely recognized, as also was the need to learn from ecological principles. Learning how to work with, rather than against, nature led to greater levels of well-being, for both human and non-human communities.

This scenario came about because a concerted effort was made at all levels of society to resolve the issues posed by climate change, peak oil and limits to growth in a creative and sustainable way.

Further thoughts

These four scenarios attempt to capture some of the broad possibilities that may lie ahead. They should be seen as only one set of outline maps, with the detail yet to be filled in. Only time will fill in the details, so further outline maps will be needed (Brahic, 2013). However, the generic nature of this set, as suggested by their titles, might well prove useful. Much is missing from the scenarios. No reference is made to the global scene, to what is happening elsewhere that might impact on these scenarios. Little mention is made of governance, which would seem crucial in any discussion of future change. It is often argued that the political time-frame of a period in government, between elections, is far too brief for any long-term planning on the scale that is needed in the face of climate change and peak oil. As David Orr says, the problems will not be solved by this generation or the next. *The paramount educational task is to prepare society for a creative collective journey towards a post-carbon future rather than possible descent into confusion and chaos.*

Governments follow their own political agendas, which arise out of their underpinning ideologies (see the Introduction). These can differ greatly in their views of human nature and in relation to what is seen as normal, right or best for society. They differ, too, in their analyses of what the major problems might be, how they arose and how they might best be solved. Most governments tend to blame the preceding regime for any current problems they face. It has been suggested that the scale of energy and resources needed to create a post-carbon society would be akin to that needed to win World War Two. In those difficult days in the UK, a true coalition government was required to achieve that end, where members worked together for the common good even though they bickered over detail. A widely travelled friend observed that regimes run by benign despots might find it easier to make the change to a post-carbon society than a country based on democratic principles. But governments are only part of the story.

The growth in social and environmental awareness that has occurred globally over the last forty years has coalesced around the sustainability movement. I use the term 'movement' in the sense of a slow worldwide shift in consciousness towards the need for fundamental change in our relationships with each other and our planet. Although internationally, for example at Copenhagen in 2009 and Rio in 2012, governments have been unable to agree on a common course of action over climate change or issues of sustainability, debate and action is nevertheless widespread. The multiple discussions and actions of NGOs, citizens' groups, networks, city councils and innumerable other groups around the world are legion. They are diverse in their analysis and focus, but they indicate a healthy system beginning to shift its *modus operandi* as it increasingly picks up urgent warning signals.

I am constantly reminded of this in my research and writing and am indebted to innumerable initiatives and sources, many of which are referred to in these pages. For one excellent overview of what has been achieved so far see *The Top 50 Sustainability Books* (Visser, 2009a) and *Landmarks for Sustainability* (Visser, 2009b). In terms of personal journeys I greatly enjoyed *The Geography of Hope* (Turner, 2008), in which Canadian journalist and writer Chris Turner explores numerous initiatives he visited around the world relating to sustainable energy, transport, housing, design and community. He writes about the need for a trail to be blazed over difficult terrain:

> A trickier mission, worth doing only if you accept a few very compelling points. First among these is that the destination at the end of it is a world worth building, a future worth dreaming of, a place of hope. Its bottom line – clean air and water, limitless pollution-free energy, good nutritious food, liveable communities worth investing in, a deliberate and fulfilling life – beats any bottom

line I've heard of. The second – probably the more important – point is that we don't actually have a choice, unless you consider rendering the planet unfit for life a viable option.

But finally – and here's the real crux of it, the thing that puts the bounce in the step of the ones already on the path – there is the chance to be part of possibly the greatest project in the history of civilisation, to be at the forefront of the generation that confronted the worst conflagration the world has ever seen – and sorted it out.

(Turner, 2008: 8–9)

Post-carbon living

The term 'post-carbon living' is relatively new, but a sustainable society has by definition to be a zero carbon one. Perhaps it is too soon yet to talk of a post-carbon society, since it is already a major step to talk about even a low carbon society. 'Low' is somehow easier than 'zero' to comprehend in this context and less threatening. In terms of the terminology used in this book, however, it seemed important that one leapt over low carbon to arrive at the goal of a post-carbon society. Its appeal lies in the fact that it speaks of a future where carbon use and emissions are a thing of the past. This is why I admire the work of organizations such as the Post Carbon Institute (2013), which maps out the contours of the terrain that lies ahead in *The Post Carbon Reader* (Heinberg and Lerch, 2010).

The notion of a post-carbon society may well be an affront to those who believe that 'business as usual' or 'techno-stability' will still triumph. The best that might be achieved is some version of techno-stability but it might turn out to be a low-tech version of sustainable transition that eventually emerges. Whichever way, our children need to be prepared for life in a society that will very different from today. On a lighter note it may well be worth considering Post-Carbon Living's (2013) ten steps as set out in Box 10.2.

Box 10.2 – Ten steps to post-carbon living

This post-carbon life is not environmentalism. It isn't 'green'. It isn't 'eco' this or that. This isn't a 'lifestyle' choice. It is just how life *will* be. The post-carbon life is an inspirational glimpse of the future ... a vision that will be here quicker than you think.

Organise – the first step. Change your mind. Study the evidence, think about the future, decide to do something. Measure your carbon footprint. How dependent are you on oil?

Powerdown – step two. Switch things off. Cut your standby. Don't leave lights on. Learn some simple self-discipline. Imagine sky-high food and energy costs.

Recycle – step three. Tackle consumption of stuff with re-use, repair, respect and recycling. Pride yourself on how little you dispose of. Have an empty bin.

Substitute – step four. Simply swap old fashioned things for new energy efficient things. Job done! No one will sit in the dark or go cold. Good riddance to bad rubbish.

Stay – step five. Having a carbon neutral home is easy. But it all goes wrong when you step foot out the front door. Why are we travel-crazy? Try staying at home.

Generate – step six. Become your own power station. Why be a slave to the grid and outdated energy infrastructure? Break free. Get independence. Get security. Generate from your rooftop.

Grow – step seven. Break free of the supermarket. Grow your own fruit and veg. Enjoy the exercise and peace in gardening. Reduce your food miles to zero. Eat healthier too.

Invest – step eight. Get out of debt. It is a big threat to your security in a steady-state economy. When money doesn't grow its supply collapses. Invest in trees and carbon-neutrality.

Make – step nine. Get a hobby. Work with your hands. Re-skill. Build and repair skills will improve your self-reliance for a future of expensive fossil fuels. It will also give you a new life.

Community – step ten. Join a Transition Town. Embrace your town, your neighbours, your island, your village. You will be more resilient as a team. The more help the better.

Source: Post-Carbon Living (2013)

These might not be steps that one would immediately choose, but they might be what one has to prepare for and might thus be useful in the long run. And even if they do not appeal, they still echo some of the essential characteristics of a more sustainable society. It is no wonder that many people might be affrighted by such suggestions, although they would have been familiar to our grandparents or great grandparents. Perhaps the degree of fear or denial is in direct proportion to the distance we have strayed from the recognition that the well-being of the Earth's life-support systems is fundamental to everything we do.

Chapter 11

Tasks for educators

The default model

The default mode for mainstream education today is the neoliberal version described in the introduction of this book. As the dominant ideology in the West, neoliberal values – the stress on individual freedom above all else, the need for constant competition, objection to state 'interference' and the dominance of free-market economics – are replicated throughout society and largely taken as the norm. Schools over the last thirty years have imbibed many of these values, seeing the privatization of education (with the introduction of Free schools), the breaking of ties with local authorities and the push for a National Curriculum reminiscent of the 1950s. Little wonder that some educators express acute concern about the damage mainstream education can wreak. Twenty years ago David Orr observed that:

> Education is not widely regarded as a problem, although the lack
> of it is. The conventional wisdom holds that all education is good,
> and the more one has of it, the better ...The truth is that without
> significant precautions, education can equip people merely to be
> more effective vandals of the earth. If one listens carefully, it may
> even be possible to hear the Creation groan every year in late May
> when another batch of smart, degree-holding, but ecologically
> illiterate, *Homo sapiens* who are eager to succeed are launched
> into the biosphere.
>
> (Orr, 1994: 5)

In offering examples of the way in which education has assisted in this process of vandalism, he cites our common disability to see or understand that everything is inextricably connected to everything else, people and planet always symbiotically intertwined:

> In reality there is no such thing as a 'side effect' or an 'externality.'
> These things are threads of a whole cloth. The fact that we
> see them as disconnected events or fail to see them at all is, I
> believe, evidence of a considerable behaviour that we have yet to
> acknowledge as an educational failure. It is a failure to educate

> people to think broadly, to perceive systems and patterns, and to
> live as whole persons.
>
> (Ibid.: 2).

Perhaps this is too much for an old-fashioned education system to take on. Conservative views of education often seem to hark back to the allegedly balmy days of the 1950s when older politicians or their parents were at school. These were the days when children were graded as best fitted to grammar, secondary modern or vocational schools, and knowledge was strictly divided up into curriculum subject areas, still largely the case today. If the default learning mode teaches us that subjects are unconnected to each other, then we tend to see the world through the same spectacles. Nevertheless, many exciting and relevant activities go on in schools that help young people to grapple with issues of sustainability and unsustainability in the local and global community.

The central issue, however, and one not always grasped, is that education for sustainability is itself a contested arena (as touched on in Chapter 3). In a nutshell, does such education support an unjust *status quo*, or does it challenge the *status quo* and the inequalities arising from its unsustainable practices? As previously mentioned these quite different approaches are sometimes described as 'light green' – only scratching the surface – and 'dark green', getting to the root of things. The first approach, probably the most common in schools, may explore all sorts of green issues, but it doesn't question the cultural and political frameworks that have led to the present global impasse. It focuses on changing pupils' attitudes and values but doesn't look at ways of changing the structures of society – social, political, economic and environmental – that created the crisis of unsustainability in the first place. John Huckle argues that:

> Learning for sustainability is essentially about learning to value sustainable relationships between people (social relations); between people and the rest of the bio-physical world (environmental relations); and between the elements that make up the non-human world (ecological relations). It is also about considering dominant and alternative forms of technology and social organisation (political economy) and their potential to foster such sustainable relations. Changing social relations, of economic, political, and cultural power, shape (and are shaped by) environmental and ecological relations, and people are more likely to realise their common interest in sustainable relations if social relations are just and democratic. In conditions of equality people's basic needs are

more likely to be met; greed is less likely to be acceptable; and the costs and benefits of living within ecological limits are more likely to be fairly shared.

(Huckle, 2012: 35–6)

In noting these two different emphases within education for sustainability – or rather conflicting ideological views about its ends and means – there is surely a way forward. A holistic approach to sustainability education would aim to both change individual and group attitudes in relation to sustainability, and help create alternatives to the existing structures of society that have led us to this sorry place. One stance, consciously or unconsciously, merely encourages new forms of 'business as usual'. The other looks to build a new, more sustainable society, in the shell of the old.

The influence of dominant neoliberal values on the issue-based educations (Introduction) that attempt to promote alternative worldviews has been considerable, as a recent issue of *Policy & Practice: A Development Education Review*, from the Centre for Global Education (2011) in Belfast, illustrates. The articles in this issue explore the de-radicalization of development education and the ways in which this sector 'endorses, tacitly or otherwise, the very ideologies and political economic arrangements that are responsible for producing or exacerbating conditions of poverty and injustice, while simultaneously encouraging people to take action against this poverty and injustice' (Bryan, 2011: 1). David Selby and Fumiyo Kagawa (2011) highlight the central Faustian dilemma.

> There is the constant danger that those committed to 'globalization from below' can find themselves co-opted, seduced or swallowed up by the growth and globalization agendas. Wanting to effect change, they feel themselves facing a dilemma of either trimming their agenda so as to have some say, sway and influence of a reformist nature within the prevailing climate or of adhering to a transformative, status quo critical, standpoint which may well resign them to a position of peripheral, maverick influence. Do they opt for tampering with, and so, perhaps, bolstering the system, or stand by turning it around?
>
> (Selby and Kagawa, 2011: 15–30)

In sailing close to the dominant ideology there is always the danger of a 'sell-out' to the mainstream agenda, especially if this requires funding for what are essentially non-mainstream educational projects.

Sustainability wisdom

Yet there are, as ever, curricular spaces that can be colonized for progressive and communitarian initiatives, so there is room for hope and optimism. The introduction of this book drew attention to high watermark documents relating to education for sustainability, and much good practice is to be found in schools scattered across the UK. Here I highlight three of the latest contributions to the field.

Some of the best international work has been brought together by Wals and Corcoran in *Learning for Sustainability in Times of Accelerating Change* (2012). The editors stress that what we need in these times is wisdom rather than more information.

> One question that concerns us ... is how the rapid changes occurring to us and to the planet impair our ability to respond to urgent sustainability challenges. Framed as a positive question, how can we take advantage of some of the emerging socio-ecological movements, forms of learning and technological tools, in creating what we might call sustainability wisdom?
>
> (Wals and Corcoran, 2012: 21)

The chapters in their stimulating book map out the essence of sustainability wisdom under three broad headings: Reorienting science and society; Reconnecting people and planet; Reimagining education and learning. Among issues explored are the impact of neoliberal policy, children's responses to climate change, learning from indigenous cultures, resilience in practice, caring for nature, using stories, how to handle knowledge uncertainty, and learning from living systems.

Different but also impressive in scope is *Ecoliterate: How educators are cultivating emotional, social, and ecological intelligence* (Goleman *et al.*, 2012), an excellent resource arising from collaboration between Daniel Goleman, a writer on emotional and social intelligence, and staff at the Center for Ecoliteracy in Berkeley, California. Five core practices of ecoliteracy inform the Center's work:

- *developing empathy for all forms of life* – extending our care and concern to all aspects of nature because our lives are dependent on the web of life
- *embracing sustainability as a community practice* – all life is interconnected and relationships need strengthening through cooperative thought and action

- *making the invisible visible* – understanding the interconnections between people and planet in order to understand the implications of our actions
- *anticipating unintended consequences* – adopting systems thinking and the precautionary principle in order to protect rather than damage the web of life
- *understanding how nature sustains life* – cultivating a society that recognizes the welfare of future generations and all forms of life.

These practices provide a succinct answer to the question: 'What lies at the heart of sustainability education?' They inform stories from pioneering educators, students, and community leaders involved with coal, oil, water and food issues. These stories of hope come from the mountains of Appalachia, a small village in the Arctic and the deserts of New Mexico, to the coast of New Orleans, the streets of Oakland, California, and the hills of Spartanburg, South Carolina.

Groundbreaking research is also found in Bronwyn Hayward's (2012) *Children, Citizenship and Environment*. In exploring how young people think and feel about issues relating to citizenship and environment, Hayward particularly explores the notion of agency. Environmental educators have long been interested in the relationship between knowledge, understanding and action, and here the ways in which young people have internalized neoliberal notions of agency are put under the microscope. 'There is', says Hayward (2012: 21), 'widespread unease that children of the market may have internalised neoliberal lessons to the extent that they now equate "good citizenship" with habits of private responsibility and "ethical consumption" in ways that leave underlying drivers of environmental and social problems unchallenged.' In her interviews with 8–12-year-olds she found that their notion of citizenship was often one of taking personal responsibility for action, including participation in the market as a consumer.

Over the last thirty years neoliberal values have created a narrow sense of agency, focusing on consumerism and thereby marginalizing the broader sense of agency as engagement with others for the public good:

A curriculum that focuses attention on agency as a personal responsibility deflects attention from exercising our collective agency to address systemic injustice. Expressing our agency as responsible participation in a market, or as green entrepreneurs and conscientious shoppers, is a poor substitute for the democratic freedom and capability to envisage new forms of collective cooperation to achieve a common purpose.

(Hayward, 2012: 68)

As part summary of her work Hayward identifies three differing 'handprints' that can be left by different forms of social and environmental citizenship: *see* Box 11.1.

Box 11.1 – Three citizen handprints

Social Handprint and *Seeds* of Ecological Citizenship

> Social agency
>
> Environmental education
>
> Embedded justice
>
> Decentred deliberation
>
> Self-transcendence

Environmental Handprint of *Smart* Environmentalism

> Self-help agency
>
> Market participation
>
> A priori, universal justice
>
> Representative decision making
>
> Technological transformation

Authoritarian Handprint of *Fears*

> Frustrated agency
>
> Environmental exclusion
>
> Authoritarian decision making
>
> Retributive justice
>
> Silenced imagination

Source: summarised from Hayward (2012)

The handprint of SMART environmentalism reflects neoliberal, market-driven values. The SEEDS Handprint reflects a sustainable democratic form of ecological citizenship. 'Embedded justice' refers to notions of fairness related to context, and 'decentred deliberation' to wide and open discussion and debate with others. 'Self-transcendence' is the ability to think beyond one's own immediate concerns and relate to the needs of others, human and non-human. FEARS speaks for itself.

Pushing the boundaries

Hayward's handprints are an excellent example of pushing the boundaries, both in the conceptualization of the field and the way in which this relates to the worlds of young people. All three of the texts referred to extend the field and challenge our personal understanding. I am reminded too that the practice of education for sustainability in schools or in teacher education always occurs in a variety of modes.

There are situations where a member of staff feels there ought to be something 'green' in the curriculum, to do with recycling, water or endangered species, for example. The notion is that environmental issues could and should be taught in schools, where and when it is possible to do so. These tend to be somewhat predictable topics but nevertheless an important beginning. The environment is seen as something one needs to keep an occasional or regular eye on. By definition this will evoke a light green perspective on issues, not going too deep and seen as separate from other related matters.

Then there are situations where one member of staff or several feel that the approach needs to be systematized. They see environmental and human issues as interconnected and an important thread in the curriculum. This may or may not involve exploration of the notion of sustainability *per se*. It may occur in a light green form, which avoids deeper questions about causes, or it may begin to question the deeper political and economic structures that underlie the surface symptoms. There are therefore both light and dark green variants of this approach, which may be constrained by structural impediments in the curriculum or institution in question.

Next are the schools and universities that have committed themselves to a greening of curriculum, campus and local community. This is a more holistic venture, but it can still occur in light or dark green versions. The former may pay lip service to holism, or it may engage the wider organization but in a way that does not seriously challenge the neoliberal underpinning of current institutional practice, as this is as far as the institution feels it can go. Once the causes of unsustainability begin to be explored, however, things move to a deeper level and the structures that support such practices have to be challenged. At this point an institution may decide to take a step back from ideas that seem too radical for comfort.

Finally, there are a few institutions that may have been able – or partly able – to challenge the ecological and organizational paradigm through which they work. By definition such entities are on, or beyond, the edge of mainstream culture. In the UK Stephen Sterling (2001) was one of the first educators to argue that true sustainability education required nothing less than a total change in paradigm. On the one hand most educational organizations are based on a mechanistic view of education, which merely reflects the same view of society, whereas we now need a new/old ecological view of society and thus of education. For many people, including educators, paradigm shifts are scary things to contemplate, let alone be involved with.

One of the sharpest critiques of education for sustainability has come from David Selby. Reflecting on the inappropriateness of the term 'sustainable development', he suggests that this should be replaced by the more ecological concept of 'contraction' and goes on to examine what 'education for sustainable contraction' might involve in the face of runaway climate change. He also notes that 'The term "global heating" is preferred to "global warming" to avoid the palliative effect of euphemism' (Selby, 2011). In exploring these issues he offers nine propositions for education for sustainable contraction that could be nailed to the doors of our teaching places (*see* Box 11.2).

BOX 11.2 – EDUCATION FOR SUSTAINABLE CONTRACTION (ESC): NINE PROPOSITIONS

1. A concerted effort is needed in the light of runaway climate change to confront denial by moving learner assumptions, understandings and responses towards disequilibrium.

2. Given the likely impending severity of global heating, ESC needs to address despair, pain, grief and loss.

3. Given the 'powerful wave of neoliberalism rolling over the planet', destructive of ecosphere and ethnosphere, climate change education needs to offer alternative conceptions of the 'good life', combat consumerism, and help learners explore and experience alternatives to a growth economy.

4. The view of human/nature relationship needs to shift from the doministic, the instrumental and the exploitative to one of embeddedness and intrinsic valuing; from a shallow ecological to a deep ecological paradigm.

5. The embrace of intimacy with nature calls for cultivation of the poetic.

6. 'Educations' that have been marginalised within education for sustainable development are of pivotal importance.

7. With global heating under way, sustainability education and emergency education need to fold together.

8. Cosy assumptions about the relationship between education for sustainability and education for citizenship need unpacking and formal and informal learning programmes need to offer alternative and localised conceptions of 'good citizenship' (or 'good denizenship').

9. Everyone has to understand and come to terms with the fact that we are threatening our own existence. To confront this requires a Copernican revolution in our view of the world and in the aims, structures, processes of education and, perhaps, in the loci of learning.

Source: Selby (2011)

When I first read these propositions they startled me, so I knew I was in fruitful and challenging territory. They push the boundaries of sustainability education into regions hitherto untouched by most such educators – difficult regions, which we need to learn to inhabit in the face of the dangers we have created.

Each of these propositions pushes into territory one might not have entered or explored before: denial of possible runaway climate change; acknowledging associated pain, grief and loss; exploring alternative notions of the 'good life'; viewing humanity as essentially embedded in nature; embracing the poetic; bringing previously marginalized educations to the fore; seeing emergency education (dealing with major disasters) as part of sustainability education; exploring alternative notions of deep citizenship; and acknowledging that we threaten our own existence.

Equally ground-breaking work comes from Sasha Matthewman and John Morgan, on the 'post-carbon challenge' for curriculum subjects. They highlight the emergence of a new paradigm of 'post-carbon social theory', which has arisen in the face of society's long-standing carbon dependence. They stress that while the consequent future scenarios can be discomforting:

we take the view that they represent an important attempt to take seriously the challenge of theorising the transition to 'low carbon societies'. Our reading of this literature is that it offers an important resource for educators who are seeking to grapple with the question of what life will be like in the future for young people in school today.

(Matthewman and Morgan, 2013)

They observe that education, with its unquestioned support of material growth and consumerism, has played a significant role in the continuation of carbon-based economies. Traditional curriculum subjects, they argue, are inextricably linked to the development of fossil fuel societies:

Modern social theory, which underpins the academic construction of disciplines and the school curriculum, was born in the transformation from predominantly rural-based societies to highly urbanised and industrialised societies that were reliant on the extraction and consumption of fossil fuels ... In a situation where carbonised modernity is no longer possible, social theory will need to come to terms with resource scarcity, and this will have important implications for how the future is portrayed (and prepared for) in schools.

(Matthewman and Morgan, 2013)

They assert that education for sustainability has had little impact in challenging the 'carbon curriculum' so far and stress that all school subjects need to acknowledge the implications of a low carbon future. Their initial reflections on this relate to post-carbon English and Geography (Matthewman, 2010; Morgan, 2012).

This is the territory where only sustainability wisdom will get us through, and into which the impacts of climate change, peak oil and ecological overshoot lead us. These are the new challenges that sustainability education needs to rise to. Whereas once the task was to envision more sustainable futures and how to work towards them, it is now clear that we may be standing close to a socio-cultural abyss. Whatever better future we may eventually manage to achieve, we first have to survive collapse or managed decline, which is why commentators now use terms such as the long transition, the long emergency or a post-carbon future. A very different sort of education is required to prepare present and future generations for such an experience. Sustainability education can provide the cutting edge for this, and terms such as the 'post-carbon curriculum' and 'education for transition' highlight the key emphases in this territory.

Education for transition

Transition should, arguably, become a major strand within learning for sustainability. At present, while the Transition Network does have some interest in schools (Hodgson and Hopkins, 2010; Hopkins, 2011; Carlisle, 2013), it needs to know more about relevant good practice in mainstream education, and sustainability education needs in turn to know more about the Transition Network and its global initiatives (Hicks, 2009). The key elements that could contribute to an education for transition are shown in Box 11.3.

Box 11.3 – Education for transition: Key elements

1. *Transition Network* – how this social movement came about, what it stands for, what its goals are, how it works and how it has spread.

2. *Climate change* – the nature and origins of this predicament, its present and future impacts, and its forms of mitigation and adaptation in the local community.

3. *Peak oil* – the nature and origins of this problem, its contribution to climate change and the wider consequences for society of the end of easy oil.

4. *Energy descent* – the need for each community to consider its current use of fossil fuel and to plan for a future that uses less energy and is also zero-carbon.

5. *Psychology of change* – ways of acknowledging and working positively with feelings of despair, pain, grief and loss, including post-petroleum distress disorder.

6. *Positive visions* – learning to work with a diversity of people in one's local area to envision and plan the changes needed to create a post-carbon community.

7. *Cultural stories* – letting go of the old cultural story of domination and consumerism and replacing this with new eco-centred cultural stories of just and sustainable futures.

---

8. *Systems thinking* – learning to see and experience relationships and society as nested within nature/the biosphere and adapting one's life accordingly to this.

9. *Building resilience* – ensuring that each community can look after more of its own needs and that it has slack in the system in order to recover more easily when faced with problems or disasters.

10. *Localisation* – understanding that a sustainable post-carbon world will work more from the bottom up rather than the top down, so that needs are met more locally.

11. *Case studies* – learning from various initiatives about sustainability in practice, which relate to issues such as food, building, transport, energy and biodiversity.

12. *Starting up* – learning the skills needed to start up a Transition initiative in school, college or university and one's local community.

Such themes can be introduced into existing work in the classroom in various ways. They could be presented as practical case studies to illustrate different aspects of sustainability in action; they could deepen particular aspects of one's own work; they could introduce the notion of Transition or link with a local Transition initiative; they might become a topic or module in their own right or be central to the work of a sustainable school; or they might be a new whole-school initiative, or a new initiative developed jointly by a school and local group – or they could be any of these, with several schools working together.

There is also much useful material in *The Handbook of Sustainability Literacy* (Stibbe, 2009), valuable both for its breadth and depth. Stephen Quilley, for example, considers the skills needed for a post-fossil-fuel age, noting that transition implies radical discontinuity and upheaval. He points out that: 'Two central and related features of the post-petroleum age will be the reversal of twentieth-century mechanisation and automation and the collapse of energy-intensive farming and food provisioning systems' (Quilley, 2009:45). Many of the required skills will be old/new artisan craft skills, from woodland, field and building to workshop, textile and domestic crafts. To these he adds repair, maintenance and salvage skills. Karen Blincoe believes that mainstream education can help educate the next generation for a sustainable life, but she notes that this will require a new vision of education:

We could start by rethinking our educational platform to include intuition, imagining, wisdom, spirituality and holism, as well as basic knowledge of the interdependence and interconnectedness of all things. We could teach the next generation of learners skills on how to relate to other people, how to be part of a community, how to go beyond winning or being first. We could help them gain the attributes of being true, authentic and content with who they are, at any time and in any place.

(Blincoe, 2009: 206)

Education for transition is not a job for the faint hearted, but it is one of the most exciting challenges any educator could be called to embark upon. What it also requires, as does sustainability education more broadly, are more holistic models of education than many of us are used to.

One excellent example comes from the work of Martha Rogers (1998), who monitored the responses of students to a course on global futures. From this, Rogers identified five vital dimensions of learning. These are illustrated in Figure 11.1 and summarized in Box 11.4. Together they show how crucial these dimensions are to any student-centred learning about sustainable/ unsustainable times.

In Figure 11.1 these five stages or elements are drawn together into a conceptual model of learning, which embraces body, mind, heart and soul. Holistic models of learning such as this have much to contribute to sustainability wisdom. Where might different elements of a model such as this be incorporated into your own school or institution? In testing this model with my own students I found similar stages of learning could be identified (Hicks, 2006a). They were requested to keep a journal to explore their learning experiences and to meet on a weekly basis to discuss this with myself and the group. The highlight for them, they reported at the end of the course, was the process itself – being asked to keep a journal (which few of them had ever done before) and being able to share it with their peers in the group. That was what they particularly took away from the experience – the wish that the process of sharing could be more common.

This chapter has reviewed some current and innovative developments in sustainability education that consolidate the field and help push the boundaries forward. It is an area where Transition initiatives should find an educational home. Such initiatives should be of interest to both primary school and secondary school educators, as well as students and tutors in teacher education. Those involved in such work will provide a much needed educational vanguard in these troubled times.

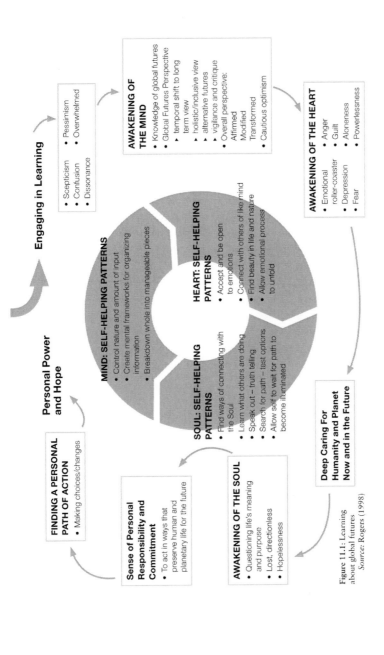

Figure 11.1: Learning about global futures
Source: Rogers (1998)

Rogers (1998)

Figure 11.1: Learning about global futures

Box 11.4 – Dimensions of holistic learning

1. *Cognitive dimension.* The first stage involves learning new facts, ideas and concepts about the global situation and its likely future consequences. Some students when faced with thinking about the future feel it is 'out-of-touch' or 'airy fairy'. Being forced to step outside their usual spatial and temporal orientations can sometimes lead to resistance. Students can feel cognitively overwhelmed, confused and pessimistic about contemporary global issues.

2. *Affective dimension.* The second stage is about emotional responses. This occurs when knowing shifts from being intellectual and detached to something personal and connected. Students can experience a range of emotions, e.g. elation/depression, hopefulness/hopelessness, sadness/happiness. Grieving is a common response to learning about global threats to human survival. These responses need to be accepted as part of a shared and collective experience.

3. *Existential dimension.* Learning about global issues and possible futures can also lead to deep soul-searching. For some, this involves a questioning of values, life-purposes, faith and ways of living. Students want to 'find an answer', or to 'do something', but often without any immediate answers. They may be faced with a reconstruction of their own sense of self, something which often occurs when embarking on a quest for deeper meaning and purpose in life.

4. *Empowerment dimension.* If this upheaval can be satisfactorily resolved, students begin to feel a sense of empowerment that arises out of a clearer sense of personal responsibility and resolution of the question 'Can I really make a difference?' Students need to be able to envision positive scenarios for the future and to learn about success stories in which individual and groups have clearly made a difference. This requires hope, humour and cautious optimism.

5. *Action dimension.* If the questions raised by the above dimensions of learning can be satisfactorily resolved in some appropriate way, then informed personal, social and political choices and action can occur. Some students report that learning about global futures eventually lead to a significant re-orientation of their lives, both personally and/or professionally. Such major choices should be acknowledged and supported as an outcome of the learning process.

Rogers (1998)

Epilogue

Threat and opportunity

While I hope this book might turn out to be wrong about climate change, peak oil and the limits to growth, three news items highlight the nature of current trends.

The ultimate meltdown

Arctic sea ice has hit a record low. Climate change has had more of an impact here than anywhere else on Earth. Air temperatures are rising twice as fast as the global average, and models could see temperatures rise by between 6°C and 14°C, depending on how fast the ice disappears.

(New Scientist, 2012)

The acute warming of the Arctic is about more than polar bears. New ice-free zones promise a rush to open up areas for mineral exploitation, including oil. The resources of the North could transform the lives of those who live there. However, such climate change has also begun to affect the Atlantic, its weather systems and places further afield.

Fish could shrink by a quarter as seas warm

Global warming is likely to shrink the size of fish by as much as a quarter in the coming decades, according to a groundbreaking study of the world's oceans. The reduction in individual fish size will be matched by dwindling overall fish stocks, scientists warned, at a time when the growing human population is putting even greater pressure on fisheries.

(The Guardian, 2012)

Changing climate affects every aspect of food supply – availability and quantity, its source and cost. This is true for rich and poor countries alike, but the impact will probably fall hardest on the latter, although rich countries may face undreamt of difficulties.

Now the climate experts warn that every house in the UK is at risk of flooding

Of the 5,000 properties damaged in the extreme weather events of this summer and autumn, more than half were hit not by overflowing rivers but by surface water. The sheer volume of rain – sometimes up to 20mm in a single hour – has overwhelmed ageing sewage and drainage systems resulting in unprecedented levels of flooding in communities previously considered immune.

(*The Independent*, 2012)

Once a geography teacher, I always thought it sensible to avoid living on flood plains or areas liable to coastal flooding. But sheer volume of rain has not been considered a likely environmental hazard in the UK before now. All our mental maps are in need of updating.

In the midst of such social and environmental challenges lie great opportunity and promise – the potential to create a society based on post-carbon principles and practices, one that lives within ecological bounds and promises the possibility of human happiness without the endless worship of 'stuff'. To take part with others in this challenge is to be engaged in the project of a lifetime. When we look back it's easy to suppose that it was our immediate forebears who had the greatest difficulties to overcome – surviving world wars, mass migrations, major unemployment, epidemics and the threat of nuclear war. We in the rich world may have presumed we were the lucky ones, born into times of plenty and abundance. Those who helped create that abundance could not have known – not at least until the mid-twentieth century – that this process would lead to massive financial and ecological debt of unimaginable proportions. We no longer have the option of avoiding the consequences, but we do have the choice of *how* we respond to them.

A new world

What is this different world towards which we and our children are heading? What assumptions do we need to work from in order to help create a post-carbon future? The exemplary Post Carbon Institute (2013) set out its five key assumptions as follows.

1. *We have hit the 'limits to growth'.* This is not a moral question (or not *only* one); nor is it merely a question about the fate of our children and grandchildren. The truth is that we have no choice but to adapt to a world of resource constraints, economic

contraction, and climate upheaval. Thus the only question that remains is this: How will we manage that transition?

2. *No issues can be addressed in isolation.* Thankfully, recognition of these crises has grown in recent years. However, all too often they are viewed in isolation. We must connect the dots to get to their source – not just their symptoms – and to maximise what little time and resources we have to address the enormous challenges they pose.

3. *We must focus on responses, not just solutions.* As John Greer says, we face a predicament, not a problem. 'The difference is that a *problem* calls for a solution; the only question is whether a solution can be found and made to work and, once this is done, the problem is solved. A *predicament*, by contrast, has no solution. Faced with a predicament, people come up with responses.'

4. *We must prepare for uncertainty.* While the general trends are clear, it's simply impossible to predict, specifically, how world events will unfold. Therefore, it's critically important that we aim to build resilience on the individual and community scales. Resilient people and resilient communities are characterised by their ability to manage unforeseen shocks while maintaining their essential identity.

5. *We can do something.* The bad news is that we simply cannot avoid hardship or suffering in the journey from a world dependent on fossil fuels and growth to communities that live within ecological bounds. The good news is that we can prepare and make positive changes in almost any area of our lives and the lives of our communities. How much and how successful those efforts are will depend upon the thought and effort we invest.

(Miller, 2010a: xv–xvi)

The Post Carbon Reader (Heinberg and Lerch, 2010) and the Post Carbon Institute's website bear rich testimony to the Institute's inspiring and influential work arising from these starting points. Also in the Reader is their vision for a 'post-carbon century', which, although brief, encapsulates its essence:

Our vision is of a world worth inheriting, where people not only survive, they thrive. In this future, we have emerged from a period of uncertainty, confusion, and questioning with a new understanding of what it means to be human. This understanding is manifested in the following ways:

- We've developed an ecological identity, a recognition that begins in early childhood of our interdependence on the natural world.
- We've redefined prosperity – wealth is counted by the extent of our relationships and knowledge, not the amount of things we own ... Businesses make natural resource conservation and local sourcing core tenets of their work, not the costs of business or a responsibility to be avoided.
- We've rediscovered democracy – government that is responsive to an engaged public, with institutions composed of engaged citizens, not representatives for hire – where equity, diversity, and a deep understanding of natural systems are woven into decision-making at all levels.
- We've redesigned our homes and communities to live efficiently, comfortably, and in beauty. People live in passively powered dwellings in human-scaled neighbourhoods. Our communities are connected to one another by post-automobile forms of transport and powered by locally sourced renewable energy. We eat food grown locally, organically and seasonally ... .
- We have achieved radical reductions in fossil-fuel use in a planned and equitably distributed way, and we have reduced fossil-fuel emissions to such an extent that, despite unavoidable climate changes, we've managed to not, as David Orr says, 'evict ourselves from the only paradise we've known'.

(Miller, 2010b: 457–8)

Lest this glimpse seems too unlikely, be heartened by John Greer's (2009) observation that such changes don't suddenly happen, all at once. He points out that however rapid major change may appear to be in history books, it is seldom seen as sudden by those who live through it; indeed, it may have stretched over several lifetimes.

A new story

'It's all a question of story', wrote cultural historian Thomas Berry (2013), explaining that because we are 'in between stories' we have lost our sense of direction in the cosmos. Whereas once humanity experienced itself as part of an organic whole and was respectful of the gifts provided by the natural world, our efforts to tame the Earth have cut us loose from that which sustains us. The progress we thought we were achieving is now being questioned because it is leading to more questions than answers. A good story, as was noted in Chapter 8, should offer clear guidance on how to do things for the best, so that the symbiosis between people and planet is recognized as lying at the heart of all things. The story we have developed over the last 250 years, which tells us that the Earth is there to satiate some people's greed rather than to meet our needs equitably, is not working, as the headlines at the beginning of this chapter illustrate. While the 'Old Story' no longer works we have yet to learn and absorb the 'New Story', which embodies and requires sustainability wisdom. This is why Berry talks about Earth as a sacred community.

> The transformation required is a transformation from an anthropocentric norm of reality and value to a biocentric or geocentric norm. This will affect every aspect of our human thought and action. It will affect language, religion, morality, economics, education, science, technology, and medicine. In our discussion of sacred community, we need to understand that in all our activities the Earth is primary, the human is derivative. The earth is our primary community. Indeed, all particular modes of Earthly being exist by virtue of their role within this community. Failing to recognise this basic relationship, industrial society seeks to subordinate the entire Earth to its own concerns, with little regard for the consequences for the integrity of the planet.
>
> (Berry, 2006: 43)

As we have seen, Joanna Macy (2012) also talks about 'the three stories of our time' – Business as Usual, the Great Unravelling and the Great Turning (*see* Chapter 7). While this may seem something of an oversimplification, Berry, Macy, Johnstone and other key commentators are deliberately standing back to take a long view of human endeavour on this planet and its current consequences. Who has not at some point asked themselves 'Why am I here?' and 'What is it all about?' Human questioning over the millennia has led to numerous religious, spiritual, social and political answers. When a friend once asked me what sense I made of life and the universe, I said it often felt as if I'd been parachuted into the middle of some complex game, with no knowledge of its purpose or rules, and that the only way to find any answers was through taking part in the game with an open mind.

I think now that the overriding question has become: 'What do we need to do right now in order to protect and repair the planet's life support system, which up to now we have been busy destroying?' Since Business as Usual is no longer an option, we are faced by the Great Unravelling, which requires us to participate in the Great Turning. In Thomas Berry's terms, we are lost between the Old Story (i.e. Business as Usual) and the New Story (i.e. the Great Turning). Where and when do we explore *those* stories in education?

In a different but relevant vein, climate scientist Mike Hulme wrote:

> I suggest we need to reveal the creative psychological, ethical and spiritual work that climate change is doing for us. Understanding the ways in which climate change connects with foundational human instincts opens up possibilities for re-situating culture and the human spirit at the heart of our understanding of our changing climate.
>
> (Hulme, 2009: 326)

He goes on to suggest some 'myths' of climate change, not in the sense of falsehoods but rather as embodying fundamental truths about human existence. Three of these myths are respectively rooted in, and embody, the human instincts of loss, fear and pride, and can be summarized as:

- *Lamenting Eden* – by changing the climate we lose contact with the wildness of nature and thus diminish ourselves. Like the lost Garden of Eden we cannot revisit nature as it once was. This myth taps into our fears of loss.
- *Presaging Apocalypse* – here climate change is seen as being about impending disaster and catastrophe. This resonates with human fears about the future and the unknown, leading to disempowerment and apathy.
- *Constructing Babel* – the bible has a story of humans building a tower in order to reach the heavens – the Tower of Babel. But the tower collapses and reminds us that hi-tech solutions to climate change may actually bring disaster.

The myths and stories reported on here are at one and the same time about attempting to paint a 'big picture' of these times, to gain an overview of what appears to be happening and to enshrine deep truths about what it means to be human. Both are essential tasks in troubled times, when guidance and hope are sorely needed.

Chris Robertson, drawing on the work of psychologist James Hillman, sees the world itself as calling to its human inhabitants.

> The world is drawing attention to itself by means of its symptoms. Whilst there is the economic pressure towards globalisation, there is another complementary process away from individualised

egocentricity towards networked, interconnected communities that show deep concern for our wounded world. The world needs our engaged participation with it and its symptoms to allow us a way to become aware of it as psychic reality. This sort of ecosystemic thinking may help us in the much needed creation of a new story: a story that attempts to see through to what might be unfolding in the crisis; a story that recognises the deep affinity between human flesh and the flesh of the world.

(Robertson, 2012: 268–89)

New economics

Economics as currently practised in its free-market mode claims to be above politics, a global venture which simply follows the logic of the market and the rational choices of consumers. However, like any other human endeavour modern economics is not neutral but reflects the values of its neoliberal proponents. Yet those who question the normality of economic growth are often seen as engaged in a public act of disloyalty to the modern state (Barry, 2012). Chang (2010), in his lively critique of free-market capitalism, argues that over the last three decades it has led to greater global economic instability and increasing inequality, which culminated in the financial crash of 2008. This form of economics, he argues, has harmed far more people than it has benefited.

The economic meltdown was not caused by any one political party but rather by the entrenched beliefs of leading economic and financial institutions. These beliefs still inform the dominant cultural ideology. Gray (2009) further argues that the notion of a global free market is based on quite unrealistic assumptions about human knowledge.

Markets are not perpetual-motion machines, which once constructed run for ever. They are institutions that display all the flaws and frictions of their makers. Not only are they liable to cycles of boom and bust; they reflect the conflicting goals and values of the people who use them. Above all, market systems are no more enduring than the power that upholds them ... When regimes fall and states fail, so do the market systems they oversee and maintain.

(Gray, 2009: xviii)

So it is not surprising that mainstream economists and financiers, who helped precipitate the financial and economic crash, failed to predict it.

If 'business as usual' economics is part of the Old Story, then where is a New Story to be found? New stories always tend to come from the margins of society and not the centre, where the dominant ideology holds sway. However, given the long-standing debate about the hazards of perpetual growth, it is not surprising that discussion about alternative forms of economics has been around for some time. Examples include inspirational texts such as *Prosperity Without Growth: Economics for a finite planet* (Jackson, 2009), *The New Economics: A bigger picture* (Boyle and Simms, 2009) and the work of the New Economics Foundation (2013). There are, around the world now, innumerable initiatives both critiquing and reinventing mainstream economics.

Some of these arise from the environmental or green movement over the last thirty years. What is sometimes known as green economics draws on the work of many early pioneers, including Fritz Schumacher, Kenneth Boulding and Hazel Henderson. Molly Cato Brown (2013) provides an interesting and informative introduction to green economics, noting that it has very different starting points from conventional economics, including a call for pluralism of views and a debate that is accessible to all readers. 'Three slogans', she says, 'can help to explain what green economics is all about':

> The first is 'economics for people and the planet'. It seems fairly glib but makes it clear that green economists are just as concerned with social justice as they are with protecting the planet. The second is 'beyond supply and demand to meeting people's needs' ... Conventional economics will provide a graph with two straight lines representing 'supply' and 'demand' and then apply this to the complex relationships which are entailed by the production and exchange of goods. Green economics calls for a richer and deeper understanding of people, their relationships, and how they behave and are motivated. The 'needs' we are concerned about are not merely physical needs but also psychological and spiritual needs. The third slogan is 'what goes around comes around' ... [which] I think sums up a lot of what is important about recognising that we live in an abundant, but none the less closed, system.
>
> (Cato Brown, 2013)

Her website is a reader-friendly place to start any exploration of green economics. Much of her thinking underlies the transition initiatives described in Chapter 6.

New learning

Sometimes new learning is about the impact of the Old Story on those we teach, and this needs to be well understood before education can really widen its horizons. The impact of neoliberal ideology on educational policy and practice has been well analysed in the work of Michael Apple (2006). More recently attention has been drawn to the impact of such 'neoliberalised learning' on young peoples' views of the future, which was the subject of Chapter 5. Debra Bateman and Wendy Sutherland-Smith (2011) consider the long-standing rhetorical notion that education has a role to play in preparing children for the future. They argue that neoliberal education colonizes young people's futures into a restrictive business-centred framework so that education becomes, rather than a public good, merely a tool for promoting economic competitiveness. Such a view of education marginalizes other values such as cooperation and collaboration, personal development and educating citizens for wider futures rather than those based only on economic drivers. When students are given the opportunity to explore a wider range of alternative futures, their learning is commensurately deeper:

> When students become aware of the multiple futures for which their education prepares them, an economic gaze becomes merely one of the many lenses through which they are empowered to re-imagine their future. Futures thinking and awareness training for staff and opportunities for students to demonstrate futures thinking in their assessment provide an innovative means for teachers to re-imagine educational horizons.
>
> (Bateman and Sutherland Smith, 2011: 35)

Bronwyn Hayward's (2012) work, referred to in Chapter 11, confirms the impact of neoliberal ideas on children's sense of self. The notion of citizenship held by the children she interviewed was seldom one of working collaboratively with others for change, but rather of individualized responsibility and action. This diminishment of citizenship was also found in research carried out by Holden and Minty (2011) on young Europeans' aspirations and actions for the future. While environmental actions were often talked about, the type of action did not vary with age – with the exception of some older girls. Even by the age of 17, boys are still talking mainly about turning off lights, recycling and not dropping litter.

The basis for grounded ecological learning already exists in a good number of UK schools, as Chapter 11 showed. The Eco-Schools Programme (2012), for example, focuses on the nine key topics of energy, water, biodiversity, school grounds, healthy living, transport, litter, waste and global citizenship. Seventy per cent of English schools are enrolled in this scheme as are 90 per cent of Welsh schools; in the UK as a whole, some 22,000 schools are taking part. In principle this might provide a base for deeper work in education for sustainability.

In their first geography lessons at secondary school, my pupils began looking at the big picture – the nature of our galaxy and the location of our solar system out towards its edge. Only then could they understand their place in space and the uniqueness of life on planet Earth. At the other end of the scale they had to orienteer around the local forest (although some slipped off home early) as they gradually became acquainted with the geography of their own locality. This knowledge and experience of place can build a sense of belonging, connection and respect for the natural environment.

Years later when I was working with undergraduates on global futures, I was told that the course had to incorporate a practical scientific element. Since this was not my *forte* I argued that the group should go on a residential field trip to the Centre for Alternative Technology, near Machynlleth in mid-Wales. For several years this visit was the highlight of the course. We lived in eco-cabins, where our energy input from wind and solar power was displayed, along with details of how much energy we were consuming. Students quickly learnt to live on less because if they used too much the lights went out. Some were blown away by simply being in Wales, which they hadn't visited before. Some stood gazing at mountains not seen before. All were inspired by the range of sustainable technologies to which they were introduced. On the penultimate day they were sent off to find their own quiet place in which to ponder three questions: 'What does this place say to you?', 'What catches your imagination?' and 'What lies at the heart of this place?' Each year I was astounded by their heartfelt responses and knew that something had changed as a result of their attending closely to this place (Hicks, 2006f).

In *Chronicles from a Watershed* (2011), Thomas Nelson and Caroline Brodie report on work carried out by postgraduate students to become more aware of their surrounding environment. This involved four tasks: charting their consumer behaviours over a two-week period and its ecological footprint; sitting for at least an hour a week in a natural setting to get to know it really well; engaging in a set of readings that challenged assumptions about environment, resources and consumption; and synthesizing their learning experiences from coming to know their chosen places. The essays they wrote about their transformative journeys illustrated the powerful interrelationship between pedagogy and place. When the heart is profoundly moved, a vital new awareness comes into being that encourages sustainability wisdom.

A rite of passage

In traditional societies life was marked by rites of passage: birth, death, becoming a man or the arrival of womanhood. These and other important events in the community recognized and honoured the major transitions in life. The elders held the knowledge of these matters and upheld their importance in developing one's sense of identity and purpose. Their observance helped the community to know collectively who they were. Such initiations have long been lost in secular society, yet such rites of passage contain great truths about relationships with others and one's community, human and non-human.

Van Gennep (2004) saw rites of passage as having three phases. In the first phase, *separation*, participants are withdrawn from one place or status to another, marking their detachment from the group. In the second phase, *transition*, a psychological threshold is crossed where symbolic actions and rituals are used to cut away the former self. This liminal, or threshold, phase is deliberately disorienting; it marks the gap between what has been and what is to come. In the third phase, *reincorporation*, the journey is consummated and the participant reincorporated into the group. As a consequence the participant is reborn, with a 'new' identity and status.

Such a rite of passage can be dramatic, testing and profoundly insightful. It is not to be forgotten and neither will it be. And it gives a new found strength, insight and acknowledgement of one's path in life. A contemporary example of such an experience, based on older practices, would be the 'vision quest', in which participants spend time alone in a wilderness area so they are present to, and can learn from, the natural world.

Life passages are powerful in their own right, but we don't always feel prepared for them. When I had to tell my father of my mother's death I realized that nothing had prepared me for that moment. Once there would have been elders to guide and encourage one through whatever had to be faced. Now older members of society are too often seen as redundant, disrespected and an economic burden. But this disrespect is part of our Old Story. What we need to reclaim in these times are the even *older* stories enshrined in indigenous wisdom. How would our ancestors and our ancestors' ancestors have dealt with these current times? Well, they did not wish to conquer nature or have the hubris to think they could become like the gods. They acknowledged the primacy of the natural world and their place in it. They learnt from it and about it, and they respected it. From this all else sprang. These are key elements in the New Story too.

It seems now that we are collectively approaching a cultural and historical rite of passage in relation to climate change, peak oil and limits to growth, a predicament that we and our forebears unwittingly helped create. The two options we seem to be faced with are collapse or managed descent to a post-carbon society. We therefore need new rites of passage to help us survive this 'post-carbon transition', many of the elements of which have been set out by Macy and Johnstone (2012). An outline framework to illustrate this is shown in Table 11.1.

Table 11.1: The Post-carbon transition

	First Stage	**Second Stage**	**Third Stage**
Sequence	BEFORE	LIMINAL	AFTER
Thomas Berry	Old Story	Loss of Story	New Story
Joanna Macy	Business as Usual	Great Unravelling	Great Turning
Lifestyle	High-Carbon Life	Letting Go	Post-Carbon Life

Source: Author

Culturally we are now in the first stage, the old story of 'business as usual' and high carbon lifestyles. The longer we stay in this stage the more difficult the other stages become. Culturally, an increasing number of people are beginning to face the second stage of questioning and consequent disorientation. The Old Story no longer works and things are beginning to unravel, but before one can move on one has to consciously reject the old. Culturally, a significant but growing minority are already working to map out and build the third stage of post-carbon living. I believe that this process could be greatly strengthened by the creation of individual/group rites of passage to mark this 'post-carbon transition'. Such rites need to change head, heart and spirit before the work can be truly accomplished. The overall task will not be completed by the current generation, but one of our specific tasks is to prepare the younger generation for these changes – and thus the great responsibility of being a teacher or tutor, parent, aunt, uncle or grandparent in these turbulent times.

I trust that in these pages you will find inspiration, hope and courage to undertake this exciting journey. Life is often a struggle, so it might as well be for something worthwhile. 'What if', asks John Barry (2012), 'we are the people we've been waiting for?' Perhaps the poet Gary Snyder (1975) captures the essence of it all in his poem 'For the Children':

... to climb these coming crests
one word to you
to you and your children:
stay together
learn the flowers
go light

References

Action Aid (2009) *Power Down: A climate change toolkit for primary schools.* Chard: Action Aid.

Action for Sustainable Living (2012) Online. www.afsl.org.uk/what-we-do/ (accessed 3 September 2013).

Antidote (2003) *The Emotional Literacy Handbook: Promoting whole-school Strategies.* London: David Fulton.

Apple, M. (2006) *Educating the 'Right' Way: Markets, standards, God and inequality.* London: RoutledgeFalmer.

Archer, D. (2009) *The Long Thaw.* Princeton, NJ: Princeton University Press.

Ashden Awards (2013) Online. www.ashden.org (accessed 3 September 2013).

Ashden Awards (2013) South Farnborough Infants School. Online. www.ashden.org/winners/farnborough13 (accessed 20 October 2013).

Association for the Study of Peak Oil & Gas (ASPO) (2008) 'Oil discovery and production: the growing gap'. *ASPO Ireland Newsletter*, No. 96, December.

—— (2013) Online. www.peakoil.net (accessed 3 September 2013).

Australian Psychological Society (2013). Online. www.psychology.org.au/ publications/tip_sheets/climate/ (accessed 3 September 2013).

Bardi, U. (2011) *The Limits to Growth Revisited.* New York: Springer.

Bardwell, L. (1991) 'Success stories: Imagery by example'. *Journal of Environmental Education*, 23, 5–10.

Barnatt, C. (2012) *25 Things You Need to Know About the Future.* London: Constable.

Barry, J. (2012) *The Politics of Actually Existing Unsustainability: Human flourishing in a climate-changed, carbon-constrained world.* Oxford: Oxford University Press.

Bateman, D. (2012) 'Transforming teachers' temporalities: futures in an Australian Classroom'. *Futures*, 44, 14–23.

—— and Sutherland-Smith, W. (2011) 'Neoliberalising learning: Generating alternate futures consciousness'. *Social Alternatives*, 30 (4), 32–7.

Bell, W. (1993) 'Why we should care about future generations'. In Didsbury, H. (ed.) *The Years Ahead.* Bethesda, MD: World Future Society.

—— (2010) *Foundations of Futures Studies.* 2 vols. New Brunswick, NJ: Transaction Publishers.

Benn, M. (2011) *School Wars: The battle for Britain's education.* London: Verso.

Berners-Lee, M. and Clark, D. (2013) *The Burning Question: We can't burn half the world's oil, coal and gas. So how do we quit?* London: Profile Books.

Berry, T. (2006) *Evening Thoughts: Reflecting on Earth as a sacred community.* San Francisco: Sierra Club Books.

—— (2013) Online. www.thomasberry.org (accessed 3 September 2013).

Bird, C. (2010) *Local Sustainable Homes: How to make them happen in your Community.* Dartington: Transition Books.

Blincoe, K. (2009) 'Re-educating the person'. In Stibbe (2009).

Boulding, E. (1994) 'Image and action in peace building'. In: Hicks (ed.) *Preparing for the Future: Notes and queries for concerned educators*. London: Adamantine Press.

Boyle, D. and Simms, A. (2009) *The New Economics: A bigger picture*. London: Earthscan.

Brahic, C. (2013) Pictures of Earth 2100, *New Scientist*, 5 October, 8–9.

Bridge, G. and Wood, A. (2010) 'Less is more: Spectres of scarcity and the politics of resource access in the upstream oil sector'. *Geoforum*, 41, 565–76.

Brooks, M. (2013) 'Frack to the future'. *New Scientist*, 10 August, 36–40.

Bryan, A. (2011) 'Another cog in the anti-politics machine? The "de-clawing" of development education'. *Policy & Practice: A Development Education Review*. Issue 12, 1–14.

Buchan, D. (2010) *The Rough Guide to the Energy Crisis*. London: Rough Guides.

Carlisle, I. (2013) 'Schools in Transition'. Online. www.transitionnetwork.org/support/education/schools-transition (accessed 3 September 2013).

Carrington, D. (2012) 'Osborne in bid to slash spending on windfarms'. *The Observer*, 3 June.

Cato Brown, M. (2013) Online. www.gaianeconomics.org/molly.htm (accessed 3 September 2013).

Centre for Global Education (2011) *Policy & Practice: A Development Education Review*. Issue 12.

Chamberlin, S. (2009) *The Transition Timeline*. Dartington: Green Books.

Chang, H-J. (2010) *23 Things They Don't Tell You About Capitalism*. London: Allen Lane.

Circle Time (2013) Online. www.circle-time.co.uk (accessed 3 September 2013).

Click Green (2010) 'Radical new sustainable house build completed in UK'. Online. www.clickgreen.org.uk/product/directory/121277-radical-new-sustainable-house-build-completed-in-uk.html (accessed 3 September 2013).

Climate South West (2013) Online. http://climatesouthwest.org/home (accessed 3 September 2013).

Cohen, S. (2001) *States of Denial: Knowing about atrocities and suffering*. Cambridge: Polity Press.

Cole, S. (2002) 'Global issues and futures for planners'. In: Dator (2002), 243–63.

Coyle, K. and Susteren, L. (2012) *The Psychological Effects of Global Warming on the United States and Why the US Mental Health Care System is Not Adequately Prepared*. Merrifield, VA: National Wildlife Federation. Online. www.climateaccess.org/resource/psychological-effects-global-warming-united-states-and-why-us-mental-health-care-system-not (accessed 3 September 2013).

Dator, J. (2002) (ed.) *Advancing Futures: Future studies in higher education*. Westport, CT: Praeger.

—— (2005) 'Foreword'. In Slaughter (2005), Vol. 1.

—— (2006) 'From futures workshops to envisioning alternative futures'. *Knowledge Base of Futures Studies*, Vol. 2, Part 2. CD-ROM. Brisbane: Foresight International. Online. www.foresightinternational.com.au/ (accessed 3 September 2013).

DCSF (2008) *Planning a Sustainable School*. London: Department for Children Schools and Families. Online. www.education.gov.uk/publications/eOrderingDownload/planning_a_sustainable_school.pdf (accessed 3 September 2013).

DEA/Ipsos MORI (2009a) *Young People's Experiences of Global Learning*. London: Think Global.

DEA/Ipsos MORI (2009b) *Teachers' Attitudes to Global Learning*. London: Think Global.

DEFRA (2012) *UK Climate Change Risk Assessment: Government Report*. London: HMSO. Online. www.defra.gov.uk/publications/files/pb13698-climate-risk-assessment.pdf (accessed 3 September 2013).

Dennis, K. and Urry, J. (2009) *After the Car*. Cambridge: Polity.

Devine-Wright, P., Devine-Wright, H. and Fleming, P. (2004) 'Situational influences upon children's beliefs about global warming and energy'. *Environmental Education Research*, 10, 493–506.

DFE (2011a) *The Framework for the National Curriculum: A Report by the Expert Panel for the National Curriculum Review*. London: Department for Education. Online. www.education.gov.uk/publications/eOrderingDownload/NCR-Expert%20Panel%20Report.pdf (accessed 3 September 2013).

—— (2011b) 'The school curriculum: aims, values and purposes'. Online. www.education.gov.uk/schools/teachingandlearning/curriculum/b00199676/aims-values-and-purposes/values (accessed 3 September 2013).

Diamond, J. (2006) *Collapse: How societies choose to fail or succeed*. London: Penguin.

Eco-Schools Programme (2013) Online. www.keepbritaintidy.org/EcoSchools (accessed 3 September 2013).

Education Scotland (2013) 'Schools Global Footprint'. Online. www.ltscotland.org.uk/schoolsglobalfootprint/index.asp (accessed 3 September 2013).

Elgin, D. (2010) *Voluntary Simplicity*. New York: Harper.

Elliott, A. and Urry, J. (2010) *Mobile Lives*. London: Routledge.

Energy Saving Trust (2013) Online. www.energysavingtrust.org.uk/ (accessed 3 September 2013).

Forum for the Future (2013) 'Climate Futures'. Online. www.forumforthefuture.org/project/climate-futures/overview (accessed 3 September 2013).

Freire, P. (2004) *Pedagogy of Hope*. London: Continuum.

Fritze, J., Blashki, G., Burke, S. and Wiseman, J. (2008) 'Hope, despair and transformation: Climate change and the promotion of mental health and wellbeing'. *International Journal of Mental Health Systems*, 2, 13. Online. www.biomedcentral.com/content/pdf/1752-4458-2-13.pdf (accessed 3 September 2013).

Galtung, J. (1976) 'The future: a forgotten dimension'. In Ornauer, Wiberg, Sicinski and Galtung, J. (1976), 45–120.

Gardner, G. and Prugh, T. (2008) 'Seeding the sustainable economy'. In: Worldwatch Institute (ed.) *State of the World 2008: Ideas and opportunities for sustainable economies*. London: Earthscan.

Global Footprint Network (2013) 'Earth Overshoot day is coming!' Online. www.footprintnetwork.org (accessed 3 September 2013).

Goleman, D., Bennett, L. and Barlow, Z. (2012) *Ecoliterate: How educators are cultivating emotional, social, and ecological intelligence.* San Francisco: Jossey-Bass.

Goodall, C. (2010) *How to Live a Low-carbon Life.* London: Earthscan.

Goodwin, B. (2007) *Using Political Ideas.* 5th edition. Chichester: John Wiley.

Gough, N. (1990) 'Futures in Australian education: Tacit, token and taken for Granted'. *Futures*, 22, 298–310.

Gray, J. (2009) *False Dawn: The delusions of global capitalism.* London: Granta.

Great Turning Times (2013) Online. www.facilitationforlifeonearth.org/great-turning-times.html (accessed 3 September 2013).

Greer, J. (2009) *The Ecotechnic Future: Envisioning a post-peak world.* Gabriola Island: New Society Publishers.

Guardian, The (2009a) 'Oil production peak could be reached before 2020'. 9 October.

—— (2009b) 'Whistleblower: key oil figures were distorted by US pressure'. 9 November.

—— (2010) 'Case for saving species more powerful than climate change', 22 May.

—— (2012) 'Fish could shrink by a quarter as seas warm'. 1 October.

—— (2013) 'US "dark money" funds climate sceptics'. 15 February.

Hansen, J. (2011) *Storms of my Grandchildren.* London: Bloomsbury.

Harrabin, R. (2013) 'UK must adapt for weather extremes, says Environment Agency'. 4 March. Online. www.bbc.co.uk/news/science-environment-21651067 (accessed 3 September 2013).

Harvey, D. (2005) *A Brief History of Neoliberalism.* Oxford: Oxford University Press.

Hayward, B. (2012) *Children, Citizenship and Environment: Nurturing a democratic imagination in a changing world.* London: Earthscan/Routledge.

Heinberg, R. (2005) *The Party's Over: Oil, war and the fate of industrial societies.* Forest Row, West Sussex: Clairview Books.

—— (2007) *Peak Everything: Waking up to the century of decline in Earth's Resources.* Forest Row, West Sussex: Clairview Books.

—— (2011) *The End of Growth: Adapting to our new economic reality.* Forest View, West Sussex: Clairview Books.

—— (2013) *Snake Oil: How fracking's false promise of promise imperils our Future.* Santa Rosa, CA: Post Carbon Institute.

—— and Lerch, D. (eds) (2010) *The Post-Carbon Reader: Managing the 21st century's sustainability crises.* Healdsburg, CA: Post Carbon Institute.

Helgeson, J., van der Linden, S. and Chabay, I. (2012) 'The role of knowledge and learning in public perceptions of climate change risks'. In Wals and Corcoran (2012), 329–46.

Henson, R. (2011) *The Rough Guide to Climate Change.* London: Rough Guides.

Heron, J. (1999) *The Complete Facilitator's Handbook.* London: Kogan Page.

Hicks, D. (2006a) *Lessons for the Future: The missing dimension in education.* Victoria, BC: Trafford Publications.

—— (2006b) 'Stories of hope: a response to the psychology of despair'. In Hicks (2006a), 68–77.

—— (2006c) 'Retrieving the dream: How students envision their preferable futures'. In Hicks (2006a), 60–7.

—— (2006d) 'Always coming home: Identifying educators' desirable futures'. In Hicks (2006a), 78–89.

—— (2006e) 'Teaching about global issues: the need for holistic learning'. In Hicks (2006a), 98–108.

—— (2006f) 'Living lightly on the earth: A residential fieldwork experience'. In Hicks (2006a), 90–7.

—— (2007) 'Lessons for the future: a geographical contribution'. *Geography*, 92 (3), 179–88. Online. www.teaching4abetterworld.co.uk/docs/download3.pdf (accessed 3 September 2013).

—— (2008) 'Ways of Seeing: The origins of global education in the UK'. Online. www.teaching4abetterworld.co.uk/docs/download2.pdf (accessed 3 September 2013).

—— (2009) 'Naturally resourceful: could your school be a Transition School?' *Primary Geographer*, No. 70, 19–21.

—— (2012a) *Sustainable Schools, Sustainable Futures: A resource for teachers*. Godalming: World Wide Fund for Nature UK. Online. www.teaching4abetterworld.co.uk/docs/download18.pdf (accessed 3 September 2013).

—— (2012b) 'The future only arrives when things look dangerous: reflections on futures education in the UK'. *Futures*, 44, 4–13. Online. www.teaching4abetterworld.co.uk/docs/download17.pdf. (accessed 3 September 2013).

—— (2012c) 'Developing a futures perspective in the classroom'. In Ward, S. (ed.) *A Student's Guide to Education Studies*. 3rd edition. London: Routledge, 133–44.

—— (2013) 'A post-carbon geography'. *Teaching Geography*, 38 (3), 94–7.

—— and Holden, C. (2007) 'Remembering the future: what do children think?' *Environmental Education Research*, 13, 501–12.

Hillman, J. (1978) *Suicide and the Soul*. Irving, TX: Spring Publication.

Hodgson, J. and Hopkins, R. (2010) *Transition in Action – Totnes and District 2030: An energy descent action plan*. Dartington: Green Books.

—— (2011) *The Transition Companion: Making your community more resilient in uncertain times*. Dartington: Green Books.

Holden, C. and Minty, S. (2011) 'Going global: Young Europeans' aspirations and actions for the future'. *Citizenship Teaching and Learning*, 62, 123–37.

Holmes, B. (2012) 'Planting seeds of climate doubt'. *New Scientist*, 25 February, 6.

Holmgren, D. (2009) *Future Scenarios: How communities can adapt to peak oil and climate change*. Dartington: Green Books.

Hopkins, R. (2008) *The Transition Handbook: From oil dependency to local Resilience*. Dartington: Green Books.

—— (2011) *The Transition Companion: Making your community more resilient in uncertain times*. Dartington: Green Books.

—— (2013) *Transition Culture*. Online blog. http://transitionnetwork.org/blogs/rob-hopkins (accessed 3 September 2013).

Huckle, J. (2012) 'Towards greater realism in learning for sustainability'. In Wals and Corcoran (2012).

Hulme, M. (2009) *Why We Disagree About Climate Change*. Cambridge: Cambridge University Press.

Inayatullah, S. (1993) 'From "who am I?" to "where am I?" Framing the shape and time of the future'. *Futures*, 25, 235–53.

—— (2013) Metafuture. Online. www.metafuture.org/ (accessed 3 September 2013).

Incredible Edible Todmorden (2013) Online. www.incredible-edible-todmorden. co.uk/ (accessed 3 September 2013).

Independent, The (2012) 'Now climate experts warn that every house in the country is at risk of flooding'. 29 September.

Independent on Sunday (2010) 'Think-tanks take oil money and use it to fund climate denier', 7 February.

ITPOES (2010) *The Oil Crunch: A wake-up call for the UK economy.* London: UK Industry Taskforce on Peak Oil and Energy Security.

Jackson, L. (2007) *Leading Sustainable Schools: What the research tells us.* Nottingham: National College for School Leadership.

Jackson, T. (2009) *Prosperity Without Growth: Economics for a finite planet.* London: Earthscan.

Johnstone, C. (2013) *Facilitation for Life on Earth: Workshop and training in the work that reconnects and inner transition.* Online. www.facilitationforlifeonearth. org/ (accessed 3 September 2013).

Jowitt, J. (2013) 'Outcry over cuts to climate change classes'. *The Guardian,* 18 March.

Judt, T. (2010) *Ill Fares the Land: A treatise on our present discontents.* London: Allen Lane.

Kagawa, F. and Selby, D. (eds) (2010) *Education and Climate Change: Living and learning in interesting times.* London: Routledge.

Kelsey, E. and Armstrong, C. (2012) 'Finding hope in a world of environmental catastrophe'. In Wals and Corcoran (2012), 187–200.

Kemp, M. and Wexler, J. (2010) *Zero Carbon Britain: A new energy strategy.* Machynlleth: Centre for Alternative Technology.

Kennedy, R. (2012) *Everyday simplicity.* Online. http://everydaysimplicity. blogspot.co.uk/2010/01/change-your-life-via-downsizing-anti.html (accessed 3 September 2013).

Klein, N. (2010) *No Logo.* 10th anniversary edition. London: Fourth Estate.

Kool, R. and Kelsey, E. (2006) 'Dealing with despair: The psychological implications of environmental issues'. In Filho, W.L. and Salomone, M. (eds.) *Innovative Approaches to Education for Sustainable Development.* Frankfurt: Peter Lang Publishing.

Kunstler, J. (2006) *The Long Emergency: Surviving the converging catastrophes of the 21st century.* London: Atlantic Books.

Landshare (2013) 'Incredible Edible Todmorden'. Online. www.landshare.net/case-studies/incredible-edible-todmorden/ (accessed 18 October 2013).

Lang, T. and Heasman, M. (2004) *Food Wars: The global battle for mouths, minds and markets.* London: Earthscan.

Lawrence, F. (2010) 'Defra's joined-up thinking recognises the fragility of UK food production'. *The Guardian,* 5 January. Online. *www.theguardian. com/environment/cif-green/2010/jan/05/defra-food-strategy* (accessed 3 September 2013).

Lawson, N. (2009) *All Consuming: How shopping got us into this mess and how we can find our way out.* London: Penguin.

Lean, G. (2011) 'The greening of the Valleys'. *Daily Telegraph*, 25 March.

Leggett, J. (2006) *Half Gone: Oil, gas, hot air and the global energy crisis*. London: Portobello Books.

Le Page, M. (2011) 'Special report: climate change'. *New Scientist*, 22 October, 36–43.

Lifton, R. and Mitchell, G. (1995) *Hiroshima in America: A half century of denial*. New York: Avon Books.

Lister, I. (1986) 'Global and international approaches to political education'. In Harber, C. (ed.) *Political Education in Britain*. Lewes: Falmer Press.

Local Footprints Project (2010) *Schools Global Footprint*. Little Dunkeld: WWF Scotland. Online. www.educationscotland.gov.uk/Images/Teacher_Handbook_web_tcm4-671306.pdf (accessed 3 September 2013).

Macalister, T. (2010) 'US military joins peak oil doom-mongers to warn of world energy crisis by 2015'. *The Guardian*, 12 April.

—— (2013) 'MPs lambast Sellafield management firm'. *The Guardian*, 4 February.

MacKenzie, D. (2012) 'Doomsday book'. *New Scientist*, 7 January.

Macy, J. (2013) Online. www.joannamacy.net (accessed 3 September 2013).

Macy, J. and Brown, M. (1998) *Coming Back to Life: Practices to reconnect our lives, our world*. Gabriola Island, BC: New Society Publishers.

Macy, J. and Johnstone, C. (2012) *Active Hope: How to face the mess we're in without going crazy*. Novato, CA: New World Library.

Mann, M. (2012) *The Hockey Stick and the Climate Wars*. New York: Columbia University Press.

Martenson, C. (2011) *The Crash Course: The unsustainable future of our economy, energy, and the environment*. Hoboken, NJ: John Wiley.

Matthewman, S. (2010) *Teaching Secondary English as if the Planet Matters*. London: David Fulton.

—— and Morgan, J. (2013) 'The post-carbon challenge for curriculum subjects'. *International Journal of Educational Research*, 61, 93–101.

McKibben, B. (2007) *Deep Economy: Economics as if the world mattered*. Oxford: Oneworld.

—— (2010) *Eaarth: Making a life on a tough new planet*. New York: Times Books.

McNaughton, M. (2012) 'We know how they feel: Global Storylines as transformative, ecological learning'. In Wals and Corcoran (2012), 457–76.

Meadows, D.H., Meadows, D.L., Randers, J. and Behrens, W. (1972) *The Limits to Growth: A report for the Club of Rome's Project on the Human Predicament*. New York: Universe Books.

Meadows, D., Randers, J. and Meadows, D. (2005) *Limits to Growth: The 30-year Update*. London: Earthscan.

Meighan, R. and Harber, C. (2007) *A Sociology of Educating*. 5th edition. London: Continuum.

Miller, A. (2010a) 'Foreword'. In Heinberg and Lerch (2010).

—— (2010b) 'What now?' In Heinberg and Lerch (2010).

Moltmann, J. (1967) *Theology of Hope*. London: SCM Press.

—— (1975) *The Experiment of Hope*. London: SCM Press.

Morgan, J. (2012) *Teaching Secondary Geography as if the Planet Matters*. London: David Fulton.

Nelson, T. and Brodie, C. (eds) (2011) *Chronicles from a Watershed: Consideration of place and pedagogy*. San Diego, CA: University Readers Inc.

New Economics Foundation (2013) *Happy Planet Index*. Online. www. happyplanetindex.org (accessed 3 September 2013).

Newman, P., Beatley, T. and Boyer, H. (2009) *Resilient Cities: Responding to peak oil and climate change*. Washington, DC: Island Press.

New Scientist (2009) 'It's a green world after all'. 26 September.

—— (2012) 'The ultimate meltdown'. 1 September.

New Scientist (2013) 'Welcome to Earth's future'. 19 January.

Next Green Car (2012) Online. www.nextgreencar.com (accessed 3 September 2013).

Nicholsen, S. (2002) *The Love of Nature and the End of the World: The unspoken dimensions of environmental concern*. Cambridge, MA: MIT Press.

Norgaard, K. (2011) *Living in Denial: Climate change, emotions and everyday life*. Cambridge MA: MIT Press.

Observer, The (2012) 'Editorial: A calamitous strategy, with no end in sight'. 20 May.

Ofsted (2009) *Educating for Sustainable Development*. London: Ofsted.

Oil Drum, The (2013) Online. www.theoildrum.com (accessed 3 September 2013).

Ojala, M. (2012) 'How do children cope with global climate change? Coping strategies, engagement, and well-being'. *Journal of Environmental Psychology*, 32, 225–33.

OneWorld (2013) Online. www.oneworldgroup.org (accessed 3 September 2013).

Oreskes, N. and Conway, E. (2010) *Merchants of Doubt: How a handful of scientists obscured the truth on issues from tobacco smoke to global warming*. London: Bloomsbury Press.

Ornauer, H., Wiberg, H., Sicinski, A. and Galtung, J. (eds) (1976) *Images of the World in the Year 2000*. Atlantic Highlands, NJ: Humanities Press.

Orr, D. (1994) *Earth in Mind: On education, environment, and the human prospect*. Washington, DC: Island Press.

—— (2009) *Down to the Wire: Confronting climate collapse*. New York: Oxford University Press.

Page, J. (2000) *Reframing the Early Childhood Curriculum: Educational imperatives for the future*. London: RoutledgeFalmer.

Park, J. and Tew, M. (2007) *Emotional Literacy Pocketbook*. Alresford: Teachers' Pocketbooks.

Pearce, F. (2010) *The Climate Files: The battle for the truth about global warming*. London: Guardian Books.

—— (2012) 'Over the top'. *New Scientist*, 16 June.

Pinkerton, T. and Hopkins, R. (2009) *Local Food: How to make it happen in your Community*. Dartington: Transition Books.

Policy Foresight Institute (2008) 'Record of the Symposium on 'Can Britain feed itself? Should Britain feed itself?" Oxford: James Martin Institute for Science and Civilisation.

Porritt, J., Hopkins, D., Birney, A. and Reed, J. (2009) *Every Child's Future: Leading the way*. Nottingham: National College for Leadership of Schools and Children's Services.

Post Carbon Institute (2013) Online. www.postcarbon.org (accessed 3 September 2013).

Post-Carbon Living (2013) Online. www.post-carbon-living.com/Ten-Steps/ (accessed 3 September 2013).

Postel, S. (1992) 'Denial in the decisive decade'. In Worldwatch Institute, *State of the World 1992*. London: Earthscan.

QCA (2009) *Cross-curriculum Dimensions: A planning guide for schools*. London: Qualifications and Curriculum Authority.

Quilley, S. (2009) 'Transition skills'. In Stibbe (2009).

Randers, J. (2012) *2052: A global forecast for the next forty years*. White River Jct. VT: Chelsea Green Publishing.

Rawnsley, A. (2012) 'The frack-heads whose dream is putting Britain's future at risk', *The Observer*, 9 December.

Replogle, M. and Hughes, C. (2012) 'Moving towards sustainable transport'. In *State of the World 2012: Moving Towards Sustainable Prosperity*. Washington, DC: Worldwatch Institute, 53–65.

Richardson, R. (1990) *Daring to be a Teacher*. Trentham Books.

—— (1996) *Fortunes and Fables: Education for hope in troubled times*. Stoke-on-Trent: Trentham Books.

Robertson, C. (2012) 'Dangerous margins: recovering the stem cells of the psyche'. In Rust, M.-J. and Totton, N. (eds) *Vital Signs: Psychological Responses to Ecological Crisis*. London: Karnac Books, 265–78.

Rogers, C. and Freiberg, H. (1994) *Freedom to Learn*. Upper Saddle River, NJ: Prentice Hall.

Rogers, M. (1998) 'Student responses to learning about futures'. In Hicks, D. and Slaughter, R. (eds) *Futures Education: World Yearbook of Education 1998*. London: Kogan Page, 203–16.

Rose, J., Gilbert, L. and Smith, H. (2013) 'Affective teaching and the affective dimensions of learning'. In Ward, S. (ed.) *A Student's Guide to Education Studies*. 3rd edition. London: Routledge, 178–88.

Rowan, J. (1998) *The Reality Game: A guide to humanistic counselling and therapy*. London: Routledge.

Sample, I. (2009) 'World faces 'perfect storm' of problems by 2030, chief scientist to Warn'. *The Guardian*, 18 March.

Scientific American (2012) 'Has petroleum production peaked, ending the era of easy oil?' 25 January.

Selby, D. (2011) 'Educating for Education for Sustainable Contraction as appropriate response to global heating'. *Journal for Activist Science and Technology Education*, 3, 1–14. Online. www.wepaste.org/journal.html (accessed 3 September 2013).

—— and Kagawa, F. (2011) 'Development education and education for sustainable development: are they striking a Faustian bargain?' *Policy & Practice: A Development Education Review*, Issue 12, 15–30.

—— and Kagawa, F. (2013) *Climate Change in the Classroom*. Paris: UNESCO. Online. www.unesco.org/new/ccesd (accessed 3 September 2013).

Slaughter, R. (2005) (ed.) *The Knowledge Base of Futures Studies*. CD-ROM. Brisbane: Foresight International.

Smith, L. (2012) *The New North: The world in 2050*. London: Profile Books.

Snyder, G. (1975) *Turtle Island*. New York: New Direction Books.

Sobel, D. (2008) *Childhood and Nature*. Portland, ME: Stenhouse Publishers.

Soil Association (2008) 'An inconvenient truth about food – neither secure nor Resilient'. Bristol: Soil Association.

Sterling, S. (2001) *Sustainable Education: re-visioning learning and change*. Dartington: Green Books.

Stibbe, A. (ed.) (2009) *The Handbook of Sustainable Literacy*. Dartington: Green Books.

Story of Stuff (2013) Online. www.storyofstuff.org/about/ (accessed 3 September 2013).

Strahan, D. (2012) 'The great gas showdown'. *New Scientist*, 25 February.

Sustainability and Environmental Education (SEEd) (2013) Online. www.se-ed.co.uk (accessed 3 September 2013).

Sustainable Schools Alliance (SSA) (2013) Online. sustainable-schools-alliance.org. uk (accessed 3 September 2013).

Threadgold, S. (2012) '"I reckon my life will be easy, but my kids will be buggered": ambivalence in young people's positive perceptions of individual futures and their visions of environmental collapse'. *Journal of Youth Studies*, 15, 17–32.

Toffler, A. (1974) *Learning for Tomorrow: The role of the future in education*. New York: Vintage Books.

Transition Network (2013) Online. www.transitionnetwork.org (accessed 3 September 2013).

Turner, C. (2008) *A Geography of Hope: A tour of the world we need*. Toronto: Vintage Canada.

Turney, J. (2010) *The Rough Guide to the Future*. London: Rough Guides.

Tutu, D. (2010) 'Foreword: The fatal complacency'. In Kagawa and Selby (2010), xv–xvi.

UK Climate Impacts Programme (UKCIP) (2013) Online. www.ukcip.org.uk/case-studies/ (accessed 3 September 2013).

UK Industry Taskforce on Peak Oil and Energy Security (ITPOES) (2010) Online. http://peakoiltaskforce.net/download-the-report/2010-peak-oil-report/ (accessed 3 September 2013).

Urry, J. (2011) *Climate Change and Society*. Cambridge: Polity Press.

—— (2013) *Societies Beyond Oil: Oil dregs and social futures*. London: Zed Books.

van Gennep, A. (2004) *The Rites of Passage*. London: Routledge.

Vasagar, J. (2012) 'The school revolution in England: a progress report two years on'. *The Guardian*, 11 April.

Vidal, J. (2013) 'Millions face starvation as world warms, say scientists'. *The Observer*, 14 April

Vidal, J. (2013) 'How a warming world is a threat to our food supplies'. *The Observer*, 14 April.

Visser, W. (2009a) *The Top 50 Sustainability Books*. Cambridge: Cambridge University Press.

—— (2009b) *Landmarks for Sustainability: Events and initiatives that have changed our world*. Cambridge: Cambridge University Press.

Walker, K. (2012) 'Transition appears in A-level Global Citizenship exam'. Online. http://transitionnetwork.org/blogs/rob-hopkins/2012-09-10/transition-appears-level-global-citizenship-exam-questions (accessed 3 September 2013).

Wals, A. and Corcoran, P. (eds.) (2012) *Learning for Sustainability in Times of Accelerating Change*. Wageningen, The Netherlands: Wageningen Academic Publishers.

Wood, A. and Richardson, R. (1992) *Inside Stories: Wisdom and hope for changing Worlds*. Stoke-on-Trent: Trentham Books.

Worldwatch Institute (2012) 'Oil consumption hits all-time high'. Online. www.worldwatch.org/oil-consumption-hits-all-time-high (accessed 3 September 2013).

—— (2010) *State of the World 2010: Transforming cultures from consumerism to sustainability*. London: Earthscan.

World Wide Fund for Nature (2013) *Living Planet Report 2013*. Godalming: WWF UK.

Index